THE GENERAL
STRIKE
DAY
BY
DAY

To my father, Donald Laybourn (1924–88) who
spent forty-three years working at Monk Bretton and
Grimethorpe coal mines, Barnsley, and to my grandfather
Frederick Laybourn (1866–1953) who was a pit pony man
at Monk Bretton Colliery near Barnsley.

THE GENERAL
STRIKE |DAY BY DAY

KEITH LAYBOURN

SUTTON PUBLISHING

First published in the United Kingdom in 1996 by
Alan Sutton Publishing Limited, an imprint of Sutton Publishing Limited
Phoenix Mill · Thrupp · Stroud · Gloucestershire GL5 2BU

Paperback edition first published in 1999

British Library Cataloguing in Publication Data

A catalogue record for this book is available from the British Library.

ISBN 0 7509 2254 0

*Cover illustration: Changing the guard at a London General Omnibus Company
garage, 6 May 1926 (Hulton Getty)*

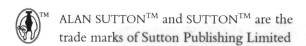 ALAN SUTTON™ and SUTTON™ are the
trade marks of Sutton Publishing Limited

Typeset in 11/14 Bembo.
Typesetting and origination by
Sutton Publishing Limited.
Printed in Great Britain by

CONTENTS

LIST OF ILLUSTRATIONS

ACKNOWLEDGEMENTS

Many individuals have helped in the preparation of this book. The archivists and staff of the West Yorkshire Archives Service have been most helpful, particularly the late David James of Bradford Archives. The Archive Division of the British Library of Political and Economic Science, at the London School of Economics, allowed me to consult the Citrine and Lansbury papers and to use the Henry Duckworth account of the 'Dover Dockers', which was deposited, as part of the Beveridge Collection, by Philip Mair, Beveridge's grandson, in the 1970s. Philip Mair died in the late 1980s and it has proved impossible to find out where copyright resides. The TUC also gave me permission to quote from its extensive collection of manuscripts, published material and photographs; the Crown Copyright material is published by permission of the Controller of Her Majesty's Stationery Office. Permission was given by the National Museum of Labour History, the Library of the TUC, the *Illustrated London News* Picture Library and the Mary Evans Picture Library to reproduce the photographs. The author and the publisher also wish to apologise for any inadvertent infringement of copyright. My thanks to the staff of Sutton Publishing, especially Jane Crompton, Christopher Feeney, and Anne Bennett.

ABBREVIATIONS

AEU	Amalgamated Engineering Union
ASLEF	Associated Society of Locomotive Engineers and Firemen
CPGB	Communist Party of Great Britain
FBI	Federation of British Industry
GWR	Great Western Railway
LMSR	London, Midland and Scottish Railway
LNER	London and North Eastern Railway
MFGB	Miners' Federation of Great Britain
NATSOPA	National Society of Operative Printers and Assistants (now SOGAT)
NCEO	National Conference of Employers' Organisations
NTW	National Transport Workers' Federation
NUR	National Union of Railwaymen
NUWM	National Unemployed Workers' Movement
OMS	Organisation for the Maintenance of Supplies
SIC	Special Industrial Committee (of the General Council)
SOC	Strike Organisation Committee (of the General Council)
SR	Southern Railway
TTGWU	Transport and General Workers' Union
TUC	Trades Union Congress

LIST OF MAIN CHARACTERS

STANLEY BALDWIN Baldwin was the Conservative PM during the General Strike and the dominant figure in Conservative politics during the inter-war years. His reputation was that of being an honest man who attempted to make the Conservative Party a party of the people. Patriotism and traditional values were his main themes, even though he had a modernising tendency. During the strike he was adamant that he would not negotiate with the TUC under duress and simply outfaced the unions. He attempted to restore the country to industrial peace as quickly as possible once the strike was over and was something of a moderate in industrial relations when compared with Birkenhead and Churchill.

ERNEST BEVIN Bevin was the general secretary of the Transport and General Workers' Union between 1921 and 1940, a member of the General Council of the TUC during the General Strike and the dominant trade union figure during the inter-war years. He was largely responsible for the strike organisation and felt deceived once the strike was called off, seemingly without any guarantees from Prime Minister Baldwin.

LORD BIRKENHEAD F.E. Smith, as he was born, was one of the cleverest men in the cabinet; he filled many government offices and was Secretary for India between 1924 and 1928. He was one of Baldwin's right-wing hawks in 1926.

JOHN BROMLEY He had risen to engine driver on the railways before becoming general secretary to ASLEF and a member of the General Council. Bromley was committed to getting his men back to work as quickly as possible at the end of the dispute.

NEVILLE CHAMBERLAIN This later prime minister was minister of health at the time of the General Strike and was responsible for Circular 703. He was at 10 Downing Street when the strike was called off.

WINSTON CHURCHILL This later prime minister was chancellor of the exchequer at the time of the General Strike and acted as editor of the *British Gazette*, the organ of government propaganda. He was one of the hawks of the cabinet and was not close to Baldwin.

WALTER CITRINE He had been acting general secretary of the TUC in 1925 and became the general secretary just after the strike, which he remained until 1946. He was an excellent administrator and quickly realised that the organisation of the TUC was not up to winning a General Strike.

A.J. COOK Although born in Somerset, Cook's early career was based in South Wales. He was secretary of the MFGB between 1924 and his death in 1931. With Herbert Smith, he was determined that the miners would not face wage reductions, or increases in hours, and was never willing to accept the Samuel Report or the Samuel Memorandum unless there were guarantees that wages would not be reduced.

J.C.C. DAVIDSON In 1926 he was PPS to Baldwin and deputy civil service commissioner during the strike, in charge of the press and the wireless. Within the Conservative Party, he carried much political power.

SIR WILLIAM JOYNSON-HICKS He was the home secretary at the time of the strike and one of the perpetrators of the idea that there was a Communist plot afoot.

DAVID LLOYD GEORGE At the time of the General Strike, this former prime minister was strengthening his power within the Liberal Party but, despite the illness of H.H. Asquith, found that his views were being opposed by both Sir John Simon and Sir Herbert Samuel. He did not think that the TUC should have called the strike but felt equally that the government should have acted to avoid it.

ARTHUR PUGH He was a steel miller and secretary of the Iron and Steel Confederation between 1917 and 1926. He was chairman of the General Council of the TUC during the strike and was to be found on the right of the trade union movement, active in promoting the strike settlement.

JOHN REITH He was the first general manager, later director general, of the BBC between 1922 and 1938. He would have liked an independent BBC but realised that the government would not allow its political and industrial opponents airtime.

SIR HERBERT SAMUEL Samuel was a Liberal who was appointed chairman of the Royal Commission on the Coal Industry which reported in March 1926. He believed that government could not continue to subsidise the coal industry but needed to encourage its reorganisation and increased competitiveness. With the TUC, he initiated the Samuel negotiations which led to the production of the Samuel Memorandum.

SIR JOHN SIMON On the right of the Liberal Party, and later taking the national Liberals into the Conservative Party, Simon attacked the General Strike on 6 May because it was 'unconstitutional'.

HERBERT SMITH He was a Yorkshire miner who became president of the MFGB between 1921 and 1928. He was a tough and bluff industrial negotiator who was not prepared to accept lower wages and increased hours for the miners.

SIR ARTHUR STEEL-MAITLAND He was the minister of labour during the strike who stressed to Samuel that the government could not be committed to the Samuel Memorandum. He negotiated with the railway companies to maintain services and to be sensible and fair in dealing with the railway workers at the end of the dispute.

J.H. (JIMMY) THOMAS He had been an engine driver on the GWR who became general secretary of the NUR between 1917 and 1931. At the time of the strike he was a member of the General Council of the TUC and a Labour MP. Opposed to the strike from the beginning he worked with Sir Herbert Samuel to bring about its quick resolution. Indeed, it would appear that much of the confusion surrounding the calling off of the dispute arose from the way in which Thomas misled both Samuel and the General Council of the TUC. The miners already distrusted him because of his reluctance to support them in their industrial dispute of 1921.

INTRODUCTION

The General Strike of 1926, which lasted from one minute to midnight on 3 May until 12.20 p.m. on 12 May, was the most important industrial conflict in British history. It saw almost one and three-quarter million workers come out in support of about one million miners who had been locked out for rejecting wage reductions and a worsening of wage arrangements. It was a bitter dispute which divided the nation sharply along class lines. It was also a pivotal moment for the development of British industrial relations and a turning point in contacts between the Communist Party of Great Britain (CPGB) and the TUC. In other words, its immediate impact on British society and labour politics was pervasive even if it barely changed the long-term pattern of events.

The General Strike began as a result of the coal owners' lockout against the miners who had refused to accept lower wages, of anything from 10 to 25 per cent, following the ending of the government's nine-month subsidy, agreed on 31 July 1925, 'Red Friday'. The decision to support the miners had been accepted by the TUC at a meeting at Memorial Hall, Farringdon Street, London, on 1 May 1926. The TUC set up a negotiating committee to arrange the reopening of negotiations and to defend the wages and hours of the miners, and Ernest Bevin implored all those present 'in the name of the General Council, on every man and woman . . . to fight for the soul of labour and the salvation of the miners'.[1] He added that 'no person in the first grade must go to work at starting time on Tuesday morning; that is to say if a settlement has not been found'.[2] These appeals were strongly supported by the trade union movement but losing some of their attraction by 12 May 1926 when the TUC called off its sympathetic strike action. At that point, there were no guarantees about the wages and conditions of miners, and no government promise that the sympathetic strikers would not be victimised. At first glance, it appears that the most dramatic example of class loyalty in British history had ended in ignominious defeat for the whole trade union movement.

Naturally, the General Strike has produced enormous debate. It has fascinated historians who have sought to explain its causes, meticulously recorded its events and speculated about its impact and consequences on Britain, British industrial relations and the trade union movement. The historiography of debate has been the subject of detailed examination in my book *The General Strike of 1926*[3] and will be examined briefly here. The main purpose of this book is to offer a detailed, illustrated and balanced day-by-day account of the General Strike, offering a summary of the activities of all sides and providing evidence of their views and assumptions during this unique period in British industrial relations. Although the government presented the strike as being some type of revolutionary plot, fuelled by communists, it is clear that the TUC saw it as an attempt to defend the wages of miners and other workers. The CPGB considered the General Strike as a revolutionary opportunity, although it varied its views on this matter towards the end of the period. Other political and social groupings, including the Liberals, were divided. The organised working class gave their whole-hearted support to the strike while the middle classes, and most notably university students, gave their support to the government, the employers and the authorities who were attempting to maintain public order and the supply of food and fuel. Some middle-class volunteers gave their support through the voluntary Organisation for the Maintenance of Supplies (OMS), organised by Lord Hardinge of Penhurst. The National Fascisti also gave their support to the government, criticised the General Strike as a Bolshevik plot, noted that there was a warrant out for the arrest of 'our one and only coloured MP' (S. Saklatvala, Communist MP for Battersea), and invited firms requiring lorry drivers to 'apply to our GHQ, when they may hear of something to their advantage'. They also published 'Our Open Letter. No. 1' to 'Parsee Pawnee-Wallah (very temporary) MP for N.B., London', attacking Saklatvala for telling lies in the House of Commons. [4] The Fascists were never very numerous but were active in a number of places, most notably in London and Brighton.[5]

Some female volunteers, many of them of the middle classes and the aristocracy, were active during the dispute, encouraged by Lady Astor. Indeed, society ladies seem to have insisted upon being photographed doing their bit for the country in Hyde Park. Hyde Park was the great food and distribution centre, and the canteens and cookhouses for the transport workers were staffed by well-known society people. Lady Mary *[Ladies help w food]* Ashley-Cooper and Lady Carmichael-Anstruther were photographed peeling potatoes; Lady Lawrence helped the volunteers to rest and refreshment; Lady Leslie, Lady Askwith, Lady Leigh, Lady Betty Butler and many other society ladies were photographed preparing vegetables and frying food in Hyde Park; and Lady Londonderry helped with the billeting of civil servants so that they might be within reach of their offices.[6]

Although this book focuses on the events of the strike there are several dominating debates which provide the context into which they fit. The first is that the General Strike was the product of an interplay of circumstances whereby the industrial tensions in the coal industry became inflamed at a time when both the government and the TUC *[Reason of GTS?]* were moving on a collision course over industrial relations. Secondly, it is

Lady Astor (left) and female volunteers

By permission of the National Museum of Labour History

clear that when the General Strike occurred it was remarkably well organised by the TUC, despite the lateness of the preparations. There is no doubt that the government was in control, and that it was able to make great play of the constitutional challenge that the General Strike presented, but the TUC performed remarkably well in a difficult situation. In the end, the TUC was forced to call off the dispute without any guarantees, and lost much support. None the less, there is a third theme which is that the General Strike was not the disaster it is often portrayed as being. Trade unions lost members and industrial passivity followed, but such developments were occurring before 1926 and the movement regained its balance within a decade. Fourthly, the General Strike was a lens through which the broader issues of the inter-war years could be viewed. It reflected the problems of the declining industries faced with rationalisation and determined that government would persist with its rationalisation policies. It reflected the tensions which such a policy would produce as a result of the downward pressures on monetary wages.

The Causes of the General Strike

The reasons for the conflict have divided historians. Essentially there have been five major explanations offered. It has been suggested that the General Strike was the culmination of the industrial militancy that began in 1910, and also that it was the product of the actions and influence of the CPGB. These two arguments are spurious to say the least. In the first case, strike activity was declining during the early 1920s and there is ample evidence that the employers and trade unionists were actively involved in reducing the levels of industrial conflict from about 1916 onwards.[7] The CPGB's influence appears to have been incidental rather than causal, for it carried little influence in the country as a whole other than in one or two communities, such as Battersea which had a Communist MP and some Communist representation on the local strike committee.[8] The other three explanations have focused on the problems of the coal industry, the determination of Baldwin's Conservative government to reduce wages and the commitment of the TUC to defend the wages of all workers.

The General Strike had its immediate origins in the miners' lockout of 1926 and the long-term events which led to it go back at least to the First World War, during which the coal industry fell under the control of

Lloyd George's wartime Coalition Government. After the First World War the Coalition Government set up the Sankey Commission to determine whether or not the coal industry should be retained by the state or returned to the coal owners.

There is no doubt that the persistent conflict within the coal industry developed a new intensity after the war over the issue of whether or not the industry should be kept by the state or given back to the owners. Once the Majority Report of the Sankey Commission, set up to examine that issue in 1919, had declared that it was in favour of nationalisation the issue became politically sensitive since the government rejected this advice despite having previously declared its willingness to accept a majority verdict. Having reneged on this promise, the Coalition Government faced industrial conflict, when the Yorkshire miners went on strike, unsuccessfully, in July 1919 and faced a very serious industrial threat when the coal mines were formally handed back to the coal owners on 31 March 1921. The seriousness of the resulting miners' strike was much reduced when the National Union of Railwaymen and the National Transport Workers' Federation failed to support the miners with their 'Triple Alliance' on 15 April 1921, a day better known as 'Black Friday'.

Black Friday later conditioned the attitude of the General Council of the TUC when it was committed to supporting the miners in their dispute in July 1925, which arose from the employers' attempt to reduce their wages. That support forced Baldwin's Conservative government to intervene with a nine-month subsidy for the mining industry in order to avoid widespread conflict. The poor industrial relations in the mining industry were certainly the spark that led to the General Strike, but the conflict between the intentions and policies of the government and the TUC provided the context out of which a wider dispute could emerge.

The immediate post-war governments were committed to returning to the gold standard. The report of the Cunliffe Committee on Currency and Foreign Exchange (1918) had advocated the strengthening of the pound to its pre-war parity against the dollar and to return Britain to the gold standard within seven years – which it did in 1925. It advocated a battery of actions, including the balancing of the budget, the legal limitation of note issue and the regular repayment of the National Debt. The end product of all this was deflation, an increase in unemployment, the reduction of costs and the decline of monetary wage levels. In 1925 Stanley Baldwin

[handwritten: Baldwin → wages to be brought down.]

announced that wages would have to fall and one newspaper commented: 'Wages, said Mr Baldwin, have to be brought down. This is not simply an incautious and inconsidered statement by Mr Baldwin, a slip of the tongue: it is the settled and deliberate policy of the governing class, who have entered upon a course of action which has for its object the deliberate intensification of unemployment as a method of forcing down wages.'[9]

Government economic policy was strongly geared towards confrontation with the trade unions. This situation was worsened by the fact that the government controlled both the coal mining and railway industries until 1921. This meant that it was directly involved in industrial relations despite its declared intent to withdraw.[10] The Sankey Report and the events of Black Friday merely confirmed this situation and demonstrated how the Defence of the Realm Act (DORA) had provided government with a battery of controls to regulate industrial relations. Indeed, in February 1919 a cabinet committee on industrial unrest was set up. It was later extended and became known as the Strike Committee in September 1919 during the transport strike. In October 1919 it became the Supply and Transport Committee under Sir Eric Geddes, the Chief Civil Commissioner. Responsible to the cabinet, it created special divisional offices in the regions and worked with public and voluntary bodies. In addition, it operated within the Emergency Powers Act, introduced at the time of the miners' strike in October 1920. It gave power to the executive, on the declaration of an emergency, to introduce temporary but legally binding regulations by order in council to preserve peace and to maintain essential supplies. The Supply and Transport Committee practically collapsed after the return of the coal and transport industries to the owners and after Black Friday, but it was revived in May 1923 by Stanley Baldwin who appointed J.C.C. Davidson to organise it as part of the government's anti-strike organisation.[11] It was this government body that the TUC faced during the General Strike in 1926.

The Baldwin governments of the 1920s were determined to keep the costs of production down, which meant substantial monetary wage reductions. In this respect they endorsed the policies of many employers who were faced with intense foreign competition, although it is clear that not all employers were willing to sacrifice good industrial relations in the attempt to control wage costs.[12]

The falling wages and rising unemployment of the early 1920s put the

[handwritten margin notes: gov. cost of production wage down]

TUC on the defensive and ensured that it was on a collision course with the government. After the collapse of the Triple Alliance and Black Friday it formed the General Council as its executive body in place of its more industrially limited Parliamentary Committee. Endorsed at the 1921 TUC Conference, the General Council intervened in inter-union disputes, attempted to improve trade union organisation and sought to co-ordinate industrial action by the unions and 'to assist any union which is attacked on any vital question of Trade Union principle'.[13] The real purpose of the General Council was, therefore, to establish trade union unity and to intervene in major industrial disputes in a way which eluded its predecessor, the Parliamentary Committee. In 1922 the TUC set up a Joint Defence Committee, later known as the Committee for Co-ordination of Trade Union Effort, to accomplish this aim. Yet it was not until the Hull Congress of 1924 that the General Council was given extra powers and presence with the appointment of Fred Bramley as full-time secretary and Walter Citrine as assistant secretary. The General Council established contact with the trades councils through a Joint Consultative Committee, with the aim of converting them to local publicity agencies and, for the first time, mediated in industrial disputes which involved shipbuilding workers, dockers, builders and railwaymen.[14]

A strengthened General Council came into conflict with the economic policies of a Conservative government in July 1925 over the threat to reduce wages. Faced with this situation the TUC gave the miners the support the Triple Alliance had denied in April 1921 and the government stepped in with a nine-month coal subsidy on Red Friday (31 July 1925). This sudden, albeit temporary, victory for the TUC coincided with its attempt to stave off similar attacks on the wages of the textile workers in Yorkshire, and also the moment when the TUC was attempting to reverse the tide of wage reduction through its new journal *Trade Union Unity*.[15]

The scene was set for attempts to avoid conflict. The Royal Commission on the Coal Industry (1925–6), better known as the Samuel Commission, examined the situation of the coal industry and suggested that there was a need to amalgamate existing mines, to nationalise mining royalties and to improve industrial relations. It was felt that the last objective could be achieved by a cocktail of measures including the development of profit-sharing schemes, the formation of pit committees, the introduction of a family allowance system, and the maintenance of national wage agreements with some regional variations. The commission acknowledged that such changes would take years and suggested that the immediate way forward was not to continue with a subsidy but to reduce the minimum wages of the miners.[16] However, there was little inclination by the directly involved bodies to accept the Samuel Commission in full. The government was embarrassed because it considered the nationalisation of mining royalties to be too expensive. The miners refused to accept the recommended wage reductions and A.J. Cook and Herbert Smith, their leaders, often repeated their famous dictum: 'Not a penny off the pay, not a second on the day'. Cook remarked, for the Miners' Federation of Great Britain (MFGB), that the Samuel Commission 'gives us threequarters, and we can't accept it'.[17] Smith added that 'I want to see the horse I am going to mount.'[18] The employers opposed the continuance of national wage settlements and were reluctant to consider the rationalisation of mines. Only the TUC, looking for some escape from

H. Smith, T. Richards, A.J. Cook and W.P. Richardson, the miners' leaders, attending the Royal Commission on the Coal Industry

By permission of the National Museum of Labour History

gov also prep fo GS

conflict, seems to have pinned any hope on the Samuel Commission as a solution to the potential conflict. This proved a forlorn hope.

The government prepared for the conflict by strengthening its counter-strike measures through the Supply and Transport Committee. The home secretary, William Joynson-Hicks, submitted a report on 7 August 1925 which led to the expansion of specialised staff, the recruitment of employers' representatives in ports, the stockpiling of resources, and the establishment of contacts with local authorities and voluntary bodies.[19] Joynson-Hicks set up contact with the OMS, which organised about 100,000 volunteers, and the Economic League.[20] Many towns developed their own voluntary organisations. Liverpool, for instance, is estimated to have had about 20,000 volunteers available, of whom about 3,400 were actually used in the dispute.[21] Haulage, in the hands of voluntary bodies, was organised into 150 committees. In November 1925 the government arranged to have full access to broadcasting facilities, and the Ministry of Health sent out 'Circular 636' to local authorities instructing them of their responsibilities under its emergency provisions. By February 1926 the home secretary was able to inform the cabinet that 'little remained to be done' in respect of the threatened strike.[22]

In contrast, the TUC and the trade union movement did little to prepare in case their actions were taken to be provocative. Walter Citrine, acting secretary of the TUC, was all too aware of the need to take action. The difficulty was that the trade unions were reluctant to give the TUC power to control events and the General Council did not receive its power to run the General Strike until 1 May 1926. The TUC Conference at Scarborough, in September 1925, refused to empower the General Council with the right to call a stoppage of work, although it suggested that individual unions might be empowered to change their rules to permit such an action.[23] Citrine attempted to puncture this complacency by demanding better central organisation and more consultation with the MFGB, the Co-operative Party and other interested parties to force the government into a more conciliatory attitude. Little occurred, and given the economic, social and ethical problems posed he declared that: 'A general strike . . . is a literal impossibility.'[24] His own doubts were amplified by the lack of trust that emerged when the Special Industrial Committee (SIC), formed by the General Council in July 1925 to maintain links with the miners, met the

TUC empower trade union not general council conflict

Walter Citrine in 1926

By permission of the TUC

MFGB on 24 February 1926: 'I could see immediately Thomas [the leader of the NUR] spoke that the miners were on the alert. It seemed to me that they were looking for something and expecting to find that Thomas was trying to trick them.'[25] J. Ramsay MacDonald later emphasised the point to Citrine that 'Jimmy is one of the most loyal men in the world, but I'm afraid the miners don't see eye to eye with him.'[26] Thomas's reputation among the miners was conditioned by his 'betrayal' of them on Black Friday and was not helped by his quick rebuke of Cook's preparations for the strike that was looming. Cook had dismissed the threat of troops by stating that 'bayonets cannot cut coal. . . . We have already beaten not only the employers but the strongest Government in modern times', and added that 'My own mother-in-law has been taking in an extra tin of salmon for weeks past . . .'. Thomas retorted: 'By God, a British revolution based on a tin of salmon!'.[27] The limited nature and lateness of the TUC preparations were further referred to by Ernest Bevin at a conference of executives (of unions) in January 1927:

> With regard to the preparation for the strike, there was no preparation until April 27 (1926), and I do not want anyone to go away from this conference under the impression that the General Council had any particular plan to run the movement. In fact the General Council did not sit down to draft the plans until they were called together on April 27, and it is better for everybody to know the task was thrown upon us from April 27 to May 1, and when that task is understood you will be able to appreciate not the little difficulties but the wonderful response and organisation we had.[28]

In the final analysis, the government had prepared for action while the TUC had not. The TUC pinned its hopes on the Samuel Commission's recommendations, but there was little prospect that they would be accepted by the government, the employers or the coal miners. The short-term events had altered little and the General Strike was more or less guaranteed by what had occurred before 31 July 1925.

Events: The Nine Days

A second debate revolves around the strike and its overall effectiveness before it was called off. Emile Burns maintained that the local organisation of the strike was chaotic.[29] Yet, at the end of the dispute, the majority of workers who had been brought out still remained loyal to the strike call. Indeed, A.J. Cook felt that the rank and file acted better than their leaders, whom he considered to be bereft of both principle and policy. So how effective was the trade union response to the General Strike? This is not as straightforward a question as might at first appear, for there are several obvious supplementary questions. How effective was the TUC in organising the strike? How effective were the government's preparations in thwarting its efforts? How seriously did the government take the constitutional threat posed by the dispute? How efficient and responsive was the local organisation of the dispute?

The national situation is rather easier to examine than the local one and evidence suggests that the General Council developed a modestly effective administrative machinery – performing quite impressively despite its lack of communication and the consequent confusion that arose over the role of trades councils, strike committees and transport committees, even though there was no serious challenge to government control. The local events are more difficult to assess because the twenty-five or so local studies that have been published are partial and deal with areas which, by and large, were relatively well organised during the dispute.

The General Council called out between 1,500,000 and 1,750,000 workers in support of the miners at one minute to midnight on Monday 3 May. The vast majority of these stayed out for the nine days. Most were first line workers employed in transport, printing, iron and steel, power stations, building and chemical industries. The second line workers, employed in industries such as engineering, shipbuilding and textiles, were held in reserve. Of these, only the engineers and shipbuilding workers were called out from 12 May, the day the strike ended. To call out so many workers was a major feat of organisation, and from the start the General Council attempted to create an administrative structure commensurate with the task it faced. Ernest Bevin organised the Ways and Means Committee (27 April), soon (1 May) to become the Powers and Orders Committee, and co-ordinated the activities of the various unions, and the Food and Essential Services Committee was formed to make arrangements for the distribution of food and the maintenance of the health services. There was also a Publicity Committee to counter government propaganda and another one, headed by Margaret Bondfield, which belatedly decided that only local transport committees, based upon transport unions, would be able to issue permits for the distribution of food. Although hastily contrived the TUC's administrative structure worked tolerably well, within the limits imposed by government policy and action.

This moderate success owed a great deal to Ernest Bevin who, through the Strike Organisation Committee (formerly the Powers and Orders

Committee, and formed on 5 May), exercised overall responsibility for the conduct of the dispute. Although his control of the situation was somewhat feeble at the beginning it gradually improved, extending throughout many essential industries. Indeed, in the electricity industry Bevin and his committee secured ten agreements to cut off industrial power in London and withdrew labour from eighteen out of twenty-two industrial undertakings and from nineteen out of thirty-one concerns by 10 May. Yet there was no way in which the Strike Committee could maintain more than symbolic control of the myriad of activities for which it was responsible.

The fact is that there were many administrative problems, most obviously with permits which were to be issued initially through the National Union of Railwaymen's headquarters at Euston Road, but later through the many local transport committees formed by the local branches of the transport unions. There was, however, immense confusion, since the numerous local councils of action that emerged were already issuing permits for the movement of goods or for allowing striking workers to stay at work. In the case of Bradford's Council of Action, the permits read as follows: 'Miners' Lockout 1926. Emergency Committee. This is to certify that . . . has received sanction to . . . . Signed on behalf of the Emergency Committee, Walter Barber, Secretary'.[30]

Mindful of this confusion the National Transport Committee, consisting of all the transport unions, circulated telegrams to all local transport committees on 7 May, indicating that only they had the right to issue permits. The telegram clarified the issue but did not solve the problem, for there was a plethora of permits circulating in many towns.

The TUC presented its side of the dispute through the efforts of Hamilton Fyfe, editor of the *Daily Herald*, and the staff and facilities of that paper. The *British Worker* emerged as the newspaper of the TUC and went into production on 5 May 1926. It was distributed by print workers through trade unions. The circulation of the London edition rose to around 500,000 but did not meet demand, so other editions were produced in Glasgow, Cardiff, Newcastle, Sunderland, Leicester and Leeds in an effort to make good the deficiency. It was produced in London up to 17 May 1926 and attempted to present what it saw as the reasonable case of the miners and the trade unionists.[31]

Despite all its efforts the TUC was never likely to be fully effective. It was not able to stop the operation of many London power stations, the

A.B. Swales (left) and Ernest Bevin walking in Eccleston Square near TUC headquarters during the General Strike

By permission of the TUC

majority of the provincial power stations or the main ports. Blackleg labour resided at many power stations for the duration of the strike, and the engines of submarines were used in London to maintain power supplies at the Royal Albert Docks, Hay's Wharf and other dock areas.[32] In addition, electricity supply was often maintained by the workers themselves as long as no attempt was made by local bus and tram companies to run a service. The London General Omnibus Company allowed volunteers to sleep in at its Chiswell Depot.[33] Ports such as Liverpool and Dover were kept going by volunteer labour.

The government was quite clearly in control of the situation. Faced with a strike directed at itself, designed to force it to provide some type of extended subsidy to the mining industry, it refused to negotiate with the TUC until the strike was called off. It was committed to ensuring that food supplies, vital services and law and order were maintained, and its emergency activities proved impressively smooth. It issued the Ministry of Health Circular 703 on 5 May to instruct boards of guardians not to provide relief for strikers and maintained its anti-strike organisation throughout the country. It had no need to draw upon the estimated 300,000 to 500,000 volunteers at its disposal. Most areas had 20,000 or more volunteers, far more than were required for the crisis, and in London, where 114,000 men had come forward by 11 May, only 9,500 had been given work.[34] The OMS and other voluntary bodies supplying the government with labour were hardly called upon for help. The fact is that the government was able to maintain the operation of road transport because the haulage committees could rely on their regular drivers. It was these regular drivers and temporary recruits who kept the special convoys moving to the docks from 8 May, and the Hyde Park milk scheme centre going throughout the dispute.[35] Indeed, the government's transport and maintenance of food distribution became so effective that by the end of the General Strike co-operative societies, nominally recognised as being in the TUC camp, were asking divisional food officers to provide volunteers, transport and police protection in certain instances.[36]

A rare insight into the government-encouraged strike-breaking activities is provided by Henry Duckworth, one of 460 Cambridge undergraduates forming part of the 'plus-fours brigade', who worked on the docks. He was one of the chief organisers of the 'Dover Dockers', better known as the 'Dover Fifty', who acted as strike-breakers throughout the dispute. There were in fact ninety-seven students who worked for the Southern Railway in the Dover docks, loading and unloading passenger liners and cargo boats.. Apparently, there was only one skilled blackleg: ' . . . Fletcher by name . . . . He was a pleasant fellow eager to do well so as to get taken on by the SR when the strike was over. . . . He had been dismissed by the Company, so rumour has it, for being mixed up in a theft which took place in the hold of a ship. The party of blackleg casual labour was composed of all the riff-raff of the town, who adopted a ca'canny policy as regards work of any kind.'[37] Duckworth's diary suggests that all the skilled and semi-skilled workers who normally worked for the Southern Railway were out on strike. Nevertheless, despite some intense picketing, the Dover docks ran smoothly and the undergraduates gloried in their efforts at the end of the dispute.[38]

The government played on the fear of the dispute to win public support and Winston Churchill, editor of the *British Gazette*, suggested 'That an organized attempt is being made to starve the people and wreck the state . . .'.[39] This claim was exaggerated, for before the beginning of the dispute Ernest Bevin had stated that 'We are not declaring war on the people. . . . We are prepared to distribute essential food stuffs.'[40] Despite occasional difficulties, the government was able to move food supplies and was also able to maintain law and order. It had about 40,000 to 50,000 special constables in London and over 200,000 'second' reserve policemen were mobilised in England and Wales in the Civil Constabulary, but many of these forces were never used.[41] However, the Ranelagh Polo Players were enrolled into the specials and were to be seen mounted on their polo ponies, in groups of about thirty, riding through the London streets.[42] The government also had little need of the military and naval forces which it had deployed throughout the country on the eve of the dispute and relied on the police, the special constables and volunteers – although one should not discount the presence of armoured cars and tanks in London and the use of soldiers to guard buses and trams.

Indeed, there was little violence on 8 May when 1,000 volunteers were transported from London docks to Hyde Park by over a hundred lorries, escorted by twenty armoured cars and soldiers from the Welsh and Coldstream Guards. The government was clearly in charge of the situation. That is not to say that there were not many relatively minor scuffles, for the Elephant and Castle, a major road centre in south London, was frequently the scene of conflict between police and strikers. Bert Edwards of the Southwark Council of Action reflected on this, noting that:

> With the layout of the Elephant and Castle with the pub in the middle and at least six roads running in: New Kent Road, St. Georges, London Road, Newington Causeway, Walworth Road and Newington Butts, it was a central focus. That's why things centred on the Elephant, because of the many bus routes that came through. The police wanted to make it a battleground. You could just say there was a crowd; men on strike might have their families with them. People would go to the crowd just to see if there were any fights. We just couldn't do anything. You couldn't control a crowd unless you had a big organisation, and we hadn't.[43]

The government's case was well presented because of its dominance of the media. It took over the printing presses of the *Morning Post*, and set

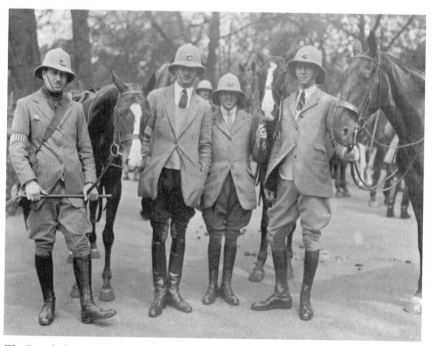

The Ranelagh polo players who acted as special constables during the General Strike

By permission of the TUC

up the *British Gazette* which was edited by Winston Churchill, who 'took the line that the strike threatened the Constitution, and at times his language became somewhat intemperate'.[44] The *British Gazette* increased its circulation rapidly from 232,000 on 5 May to 2,209,000 by 12 May.[45] It had access to facilities and paper, neither of which was readily available to the workers' press. The government also dominated the airwaves, for the BBC only permitted Baldwin, government ministers and those in favour of the government position the opportunity to broadcast to the nation. Attempts by J. Ramsay MacDonald, David Lloyd George and the Archbishop of Canterbury, with his peace plan, to speak on the BBC were thwarted by J.C.C. Davidson, acting as deputy chief civil commissioner, on behalf of the prime minister. Davidson and the government imposed controls which allowed the BBC to broadcast news from trade union sources but also allowed for the vetting and censorship of anything that would not be in the interest of the nation.[46] This ensured that views contrary to those of the government were not broadcast and that the government was able to emphasise the

Mounted police dispersing strikers after a riot at the Elephant and Castle, south London
By permission of the National Museum of Labour History

constitutional challenge the General Strike posed without much contradiction. Indeed, the media made much of the Astbury Judgment of 11 May, which supported the National Sailors' and Firemen's Union in its refusal to allow the TUC to order its members to leave work. Astbury argued that the General Strike was 'illegal and contrary to the law' since under the 1906 Act 'no trade dispute had been alleged or shown to exist in any case of the unions affiliated, except in the miners' case'.[47]

The government also kept in close contact with the railway companies both in order to keep a check on the movement of food and to inform the public of the available train services. All the railway companies held their daily meetings of managers, line meetings, railway police meetings and the like, and met the minister of transport or his representatives. Their day-to-day position was announced by BBC wireless broadcasts.[48] Indeed, the various railway companies – the Great Western, the Southern, the London and North Eastern, the London, Midland and Scottish, the Metropolitan and the London Underground – also met with the minister of transport and decided to take a very harsh line with those workers who had come out on strike once they offered themselves for re-employment.[49]

Sir Felix J.C. Pole, general manager of the Great Western Railway (GWR), was one of the most intransigent of the railway general managers. He was determined to keep Paddington station operating, published the *Great Western Railway Bulletin* which asked 'All Loyalists' to 'LEND A HAND' and was, subsequently, one of the hard bargainers at the end of the dispute.[50] Pole and the GWR constantly emphasised the way in which the strike was being defeated, noting that the number of 'perishable' traffic trains on the GWR increased from 194 to 1,164 between 5 and 12 May.[51] The GWR also enrolled hundreds of special constables to protect its stations and services, and had 1,869 of them on 8 May, of whom 557 were at Paddington, 55 at Bristol, 68 at Birmingham, 55 at Birkenhead, 112 at Wolverhampton and the rest distributed in smaller numbers at all the other stations. By 8 May it had also enrolled 5,620 volunteers, of whom 2,234 had been put to work.[52] With such activities being reported throughout the railway system it is not surprising that the network kept going, albeit at a much reduced level of activity. Indeed, the GWR estimated that an average of 81 per cent of its staff were on strike throughout the dispute. As a result it trained 252 of its volunteers to a standard sufficient to take charge of signal boxes through the provision of a one-day course based on two three-hour lectures and 'A text book specially prepared in readiness for such an emergency . . .'.[53]

The government was clearly able to control the national situation and was far more prepared for the dispute. But how effective were the local authorities and the trade unions at the local level? In contrast to the reasonably complete national picture of the General Strike there is nothing like a comprehensive picture of events at the local level, as there are about twenty-five published local studies and only one attempt at a national survey. It is estimated that there were upwards of 500 councils of action or similar bodies formed on the workers' side, although Emile Burns was only able to obtain 190 replies, 131 of a detailed nature, for his Labour Research Department survey of their activities in 1926.[54] Burns' assessment was, given that the trades councils and councils of action were 'suddenly asked to take a new and urgent task, without any but the vaguest suggestion of how they should carry it out . . . viewed as a whole it was carried out effectively'.[55] Ellen Wilkinson and J.F. Horrabin, in their speaking tour of the country during the dispute, confirmed this impression, noting the support of G.D.H. Cole and some undergraduates at Oxford, the effectiveness of the Coventry Soviet, solid villages between Stafford and Crewe and the great spirit for the dispute in the Rhondda.[56] Indeed, 'Reactionary Oxford was solid, its main difficulty being to keep high dignitaries off the strike committee!' Such views and impressions are supported by Alan Clinton, although he notes that many trades councils had anticipated their role before May 1926: 'In September (1925) the President of the Birmingham Trades Council urged delegates to be fully prepared for the coming struggle, and early in 1926 the Bradford leaders said "they strongly urge Trade Unionists to make preparations for the fight".'[57] In addition, Clinton notes that at a 'Special Conference of Action' on 21 March 1926, fifty-two trades councils advertised their willingness to take action, stimulated partly by left-wing and communist activists. Local trades councils were also prepared for action in Huddersfield, Preston, Liverpool and many other centres. As a result, argues Clinton, almost every major urban centre had a well-thought-out strike organisation in place by the beginning of the dispute. Indeed, the strike organisations acted so effectively that Jimmy Thomas began to fear that they would take over control of the strike, and they did form an effective rival organisation to the local authorities. As Clinton argues,

'After the General Strike many trades councils felt that they had done something to prove themselves.'[58]

Indeed, the trades councils and councils of action formed numerous subcommittees, issued local permits, distributed relief, organised pickets, made local arrangements with sympathetic co-operative societies, published bulletins, arranged speakers for open-air meetings and covered a wide range of activities. The Labour Research Department indicates that between 70 and 72 of the 140 councils of action/trades councils that replied on the matter issued local strike publications. The titles included the *Preston Strike News*, *Brighton Bulletin*, *Westminster Worker*, the *Newcastle Workers' Chronicle* and *The Northern Light*, the bulletin of the Blaydon and Chopwell District Council of Action.[59] The National Museum of Labour History has copies of some of these publications, including *The Dover and East Kent Worker*, the *Gloucester Strike Bulletin*, *The Scottish Worker* and the *Dowsona Bulletin*.[60] The publication of such news-sheets exceeded the orders of the TUC, which felt that no local comment should be made and also ordered the cessation of all strike bulletins on 10 May, an action which later provoked C.B. of the Communist Party of Great Britain to reflect that: 'It was a mistake to stop the workers' press, which should have increased in volume during the strike. To knock a powerful weapon out of the hands of the capitalists is good. To throw one's own weapon away after it was foolish.'[61] To be fair, many of these publications continued regardless until the end of the dispute.

Yet such a vast array of activity does not indicate the level of effectiveness of the strike, although it may convey a high level of commitment by the working classes. Clearly, the TUC had some problems, emanating from its late preparations. It had to deal with 465 trades councils/councils of action in Britain, as well as a similar number of transport committees, instead of being able to work with eleven district organisations (London and ten other divisions) as the government was able to do.[62] Notwithstanding such failure, there were a number of widespread regional district organisations formed, such as the Merseyside Council of Action, which covered Birkenhead, Bootle, Liverpool and Wallasey. There were also county federations of councils of action in Lanarkshire and east Glamorgan, and a shadowy body known as the North West Area Strike Council, based in Manchester.[63] The General Council of the Scottish TUC also took responsibility for overseeing the General Strike in Scotland, committing itself to ensuring that the 'policy carried out by the BTUC is carried out loyally'.[64] Indeed, it declared that, 'It is not our function to decide policy or to discuss the general situation.' Its problem was not to get the men out, 'but to keep those who were not asked to cease work from throwing in their lot with the strikers'.[65] Equally overt and effective were the Teesside Federation and the Northumberland and Durham Joint Committee, both of which acted with some success against the government's strike-breaking machinery.[66] The latter was based at Newcastle and had little or no influence north of Ashington or south of Gateshead.

There were many administrative failings as well as successes in the attempts to make the General Strike effective at the local level. Many councils of action had no bulletins and some, such as Middlesbrough, Sheffield and St Albans, were fragmented. There was also much confusion between the trades councils/councils of action and the local transport committees (of the transport unions) about who was allowed to issue permits. Yet recent work

Typical cartoons from the *St Pancras Bulletin*

By permission of the National Museum of Labour History

PUFF, PUFF, PUFF, GOES THE ENGINE.

From *St. Pancras Bulletin*, No. 4, May 6th, 2nd Edition.

Cartoons from strike bulletins

By permission of the TUC

Cardiff Strike Bulletin editorial staff

By permission of the National Museum of Labour History

tends, on the whole, to be more favourable than contemporary opinion allowed, pointing to the way in which the trades councils/councils of action prepared for the conflict and were reasonably effective.

Alan Clinton has suggested that many local organisations had anticipated the dispute, a view endorsed by other research. The organisation of Leeds was less fragmented than has often been supposed.[67] In Nottingham it was announced on 6 May that 'Mr Harding, the area food controller, has undertaken to move no food except by permission of the Strike Committee. He does not recognise the OMS.'[68] In Birmingham, the strike was immediately effective and it was reported that 'The extent of the stoppage is much greater than anybody anticipated and all road, passenger, and carrying traffic has been stopped.'[69] In Gloucester, the port was brought to a halt and the local strike activity was marked, while a similar picture of success emerges for Merseyside, the North East and York.[70] In Aberdeen it was reported on 10 May that 'The railwaymen solid; no trains running . . . . The local bakers have agreed tonight to stop their supplies. The docks are out

Penzance General Strike Committee

By permission of the National Museum of Labour History

solidly.'[71] In Doncaster, 'The unions are of course out to the last man. The strike committees are working splendidly and have matters under excellent control.'[72] The strike was almost totally effective in Bradford, bringing the trams and the railways to a virtually complete standstill.[73]

It would appear that the workers responded well to the strike call. There were about 40,000 directly participating in the dispute in Leeds, about 7,000 in York, 100,000 on Merseyside.[74] Most of the railwaymen came out and, on average, more than 80 per cent of the workers of the Great Western Railway, more or less everybody except the clerical and supervisory staff, were out on strike for the nine days and beyond.[75] It is difficult to gain a complete picture of the rank and file support, but it does seem to have been extensive: the railwaymen were solid and the Plebs League's survey of the response, published in *A Worker's History of the Great Strike,* also suggests that in the vast majority of cases most of the front line workers came out.[76]

Camberwell Trades Council demonstration during the General Strike
By permission of the National Museum of Labour History

Most strike committees and councils of action abided by the instructions of the General Council, constantly reiterated in the *British Worker*, that they must 'Stand Firm and Keep Order'.[77] This was accepted even when the General Council sought to reduce the number of permits and when mass picketing occurred. Consequently, serious violence was rare. Indeed, the General Council noted that, 'Despite the presence of armed police and the military, the workers have preserved a quiet orderliness and dignity, which the General Council urges them to maintain . . .'.[78]

Nevertheless, there were some disturbances. There were tram riots in Plymouth, and large and unorganised crowds rioted in Hull and Middlesbrough.[79] There were also major riots in Edinburgh, Glasgow, Newcastle, Preston, Crewe, Nottingham, Swansea and other towns. Where there was the likelihood of conflict with the police Workers' Defence Corps were often organised, as in Leeds, Methil, Fife and about a dozen other areas.[80]

The worst incidents of violence were in Glasgow, Doncaster, Tyneside and London. In Glasgow about 200 arrests were made as a result of clashes between the police and the miners. In Doncaster there was conflict between the miners and the police at Hatfield on 12 May, and between pickets and the police at Edenthorpe. The first led to the arrest of seventy pickets and the second to the arrest of fourteen.[81] What was potentially one of the worst incidents occurred on 10 May when the Edinburgh to London express, the 'Flying Scotsman', was derailed near Newcastle in what was considered a dreadful example of vandalism.

Nevertheless, as was the case with the government, the local authorities were generally able to maintain some control of essential services and foodstuffs, except perhaps in some of the mining areas. Most towns appointed officers and committees to keep food and coal supplies flowing, normally drawn from their existing administrative structure. They had many volunteers to draw upon but, as previously suggested, rarely used them either because they did not need them or because they feared the conflict that they might encourage.

The government held the rather exaggerated belief that there was an enormous communist plot afoot and that the CPGB was behind much of the violence that occurred. It had already prosecuted twelve leading communists on 23 October 1925 under the Incitement to Mutiny Act of 1797. They were all found guilty and imprisoned for either six months or a year.[82] It has been estimated that about half of the 5,000 CPGB membership was arrested during the General Strike, which was a significant proportion of the 4,000 or so arrests that occurred during the dispute, 600 of which were without a warrant under the Emergency Powers Act. In the West Riding of Yorkshire action was taken against the Communist 'strongholds' of Castleford and Shipley. On 9 May it was reported that:

> At Pontefract yesterday Isobel Brown, who said that her last permanent address was Moscow, was committed for three months in the second division for having delivered a speech at Castleford on Wednesday likely to cause disaffection. She admitted she had come from London to gain recruits for the Communist Party but denied any attempt to stir up strife.[83]

She was arrested in a raid on the Shipley Independent Labour Party (ILP) rooms where Communists, and other strike helpers, were producing a paper.

There were many communists helping the strike effort throughout the country but little evidence that they dominated the councils of action or the strike committees. There were five on the Central Strike Committee in Glasgow, two on the Town Strike Committee at Falkirk, four on Middlesbrough Central Strike Committee, three on the Barrow Council of Action, and two or three were present on many other bodies. Yet it was only in Battersea in the London seat of S. Saklatvala (the Communist MP), that there was a significant communist presence, with ten on a committee of a hundred and twenty-four, of whom four were on the seven-member executive committee.[84] As already indicated, the authorities were so concerned that they took action against Saklatvala and imprisoned him for two months for making seditious statements at the May Day rally at Hyde Park on the eve of the dispute.

The General Strike, by its very diversity and local and regional variation, presents difficulties of assessment. The Tory press raged against the idea of revolution and the government played upon such fears.[85] Yet there was no revolutionary threat as such, and while violence and conflict occurred it did not assume the seriousness so often associated with European disturbances. The fact is that the government and the local authorities felt that they kept matters well under control while allowing the strike committees to achieve some local successes in closing down the railways and other forms of transport. For nine days Britain experienced a significant shutdown of its normal life without the government losing control of the situation. Indeed, as the dispute continued the government became more confident of its position just as the TUC began to fear for the trade union movement. In the final analysis, however, it did not matter that workers responded magnificently to the strike call because it was a small coterie of trade union leaders, and not the rank and file, who determined the outcome of the dispute.

The Settlement and the Outcome

A.J. Cook wrote of the General Strike that, 'The workers acted as one. Splendid discipline. Splendid loyalty!' He then asked, ' Why was the strike called off?'[86] It is a question that has exercised the minds of historians and contemporaries alike. Cook's answer was that Jimmy Thomas and the right-wing leaders of the TUC were opposed to the strike and sought to end it with indecent haste.[87] The CPGB also attacked the General Council by suggesting that the calling off of the dispute was 'the greatest crime that has ever been committed'.[88] Others have expressed similar views, encouraged partly by Jimmy Thomas's comments in the House of Commons that the strike had to be called off before 'it got out of hand'.[89] While the fine detail might vary the gist of the argument is that the General Council sought a pretext to end the dispute at the earliest opportunity. Unlike the government, it welcomed the offer of help from Sir Herbert Samuel as the route to an honourable settlement. It negotiated with him on 7–8 May, and helped to produce the first version of the 'Samuel Memorandum' which advocated the reorganisation of the coal industry and a wage reduction for a year, but included the added device of an impartial National Wages Board to maintain a watch over the

Looking out from the TUC offices at Eccleston Square at the time of the General Strike
By permission of the National Museum of Labour History

reorganisation of the industry and the local wage agreements. This was shown to the miners on the following day and rejected by them in a meeting with the TUC on 10 May, despite some suggested alterations.[90] After another fruitless meeting between the General Council and the miners on 11 May the General Council asked Walter Citrine to contact the prime minister, and arranged to meet at 10 Downing Street at noon the next day.[91] By 12.20 p.m. the strike had been called off. Within an hour the news was given to journalists, whereupon the BBC informed the nation and Baldwin announced the decision to the House of Commons. The Anti-Socialist Union Press Service issued a statement to inform the nation immediately the decision was announced.[92]

This famous meeting saw the representatives of the General Council enter 10 Downing Street only on the proviso that the General Strike had been called off and without any guarantees. Baldwin talked vaguely about the Samuel Memorandum and made no mention at all of the end of victimisation. Arthur Pugh and Walter Citrine, upon their return to TUC headquarters at Eccleston Square, sent telegrams to the trade unions instructing them to order the resumption of work. In a later letter they circulated the details of the Samuel Memorandum. They were held to represent 'sufficient assurances . . . as to the lines upon which a settlement could be reached to justify them terminating the General Strike', a decision taken to enable negotiations to continue. The General Council later (in June) justified its position, by suggesting that 'The strike was terminated for one sufficient reason only, namely that in view of the attitude of the Miners' Federation its continuance would have rendered its purpose futile.'[93] This was not the attitude of the miners who took a wider view of the dispute and invoked Philip Snowden's opinion that 'This is an owners' strike against the community.'[94] The miners' leaders felt that the General Council should have taken the broader view and continued the fight.

The General Strike had come to a swift and unsatisfactory conclusion largely because the General Council believed that it could not win. It was barely committed to the dispute from the start, did not like the way in which its actions were challenging the Constitution, believed that the dispute could bleed the finances of trade unions dry and felt that the coal miners would not compromise. It looked for an escape route and the Samuel Memorandum seemed to provide an opportunity for an orderly retreat from conflict. When the Samuel Memorandum was not accepted by the government Arthur Pugh complained to Samuel that he had been misled and Ernest Bevin and other members of the General Council felt the same, despite the fact that Samuel had made it quite clear that he was not acting on behalf of the government but supplying his good offices to help settle the dispute.[95] Obviously, calling off the General Strike was a disaster for the General Council, but it did not mean that the trade union movement was set back a generation; indeed, the trade union movement was markedly more successful after 1926 than it had been before.

The Consequences and Aftermath of the General Strike

The General Strike ended in confusion, not least because both the TUC and the government claimed success. Walter Citrine informed the affiliated trade unions and trades councils that assurances had been given such that the General Strike could be called off and the miners' case reopened.[96] Yet it was soon clear that the Samuel Memorandum was not to be the basis of negotiation in the mining industry, and that there were no guarantees against the victimisation of those workers who had been called out.

At first, trade unionists throughout the country felt that they had been successful. Oswald Mosley announced to the Birmingham trade unionists that 'they had whipped the Government'.[97] This was not an uncommon reaction, although most trade unionists soon came to realise that they had been defeated. Employers began to demand their retribution in almost every community throughout the country. In Glasgow 368 of the 5,000 tramwaymen were suspended or dismissed. Brighton Town Council also forced its tramway staff to leave the Transport and General Workers' Union. The printing employers became bullish and united to eliminate trade union organisation in Scotland. The *Manchester Guardian* formed its own house union. The various national agreements that emerged certainly threatened the power of the trade unions.

The basis of a printing agreement was worked out on 16 May and published widely in the press on the next day. It contained seven main points, the most important of which being that there would be no interference with the control of newspapers, that the unions would not interfere with the right of the newspaper managements to appoint staff and that the members of staff who acted as blacklegs would not be victimised. In these, and in other ways, the power of the printing unions was reduced.[98]

The terms of settlement in the London docks, affecting 50,000 men, were similar, with a seven-point agreement committing the union to follow the national agreement for settling disputes. The employers were committed to taking back the men only when work was available, a situation which Ernest Bevin felt was acceptable.[99]

Yet the most obvious evidence of employer aggression came in the case of the railway companies. They attempted to force the railway unions to accept that not all the men would get their jobs back, and tried to force those who returned to accept that they had been responsible for a 'wrongful act'.[100] Eventually a compromise was arranged on 14 May in which, in return for reinstatement, the guaranteed week was suspended and the railway unions acknowledged that they had committed a 'wrongful act'.[101] There was much evidence of victimisation throughout industry and that the employers were demoting staff because of their support of the General Strike, but in the end the vast majority of workers got their jobs back on the basis of the reinstatement of senior staff first.[102] But what had they achieved for the risk to their jobs and their prospects of promotion?

The coal miners' lockout was no nearer settlement as a result of the General Strike and, despite numerous attempts to resolve it, was ended by the capitulation of the miners in November 1926.[103] The MFGB eventually asked its regional organisations to make the best terms they could for return with national standards. Regional variation was inevitable. All the workers returned on a 7½-hour day in Yorkshire, while longer hours and wage reductions were imposed in South Wales, Scotland and the North-East. In Nottinghamshire, those workers who had returned to work under George Spencer's breakaway union were given a four shilling per week wage increase.

There is no doubt that the collapse of the General Strike and the capitulation of the miners in the coal lockout were devastating to the British trade union movement, earning the General Council obloquy: the prestige of the trade union movement certainly suffered in the short term. Yet the trade unions were not destroyed and were still able to mount an effective check to the employers.

The main criticism of the General Council came from the CPGB.

This maintained that the decision to call off the General Strike 'is the greatest crime that has ever been permitted, not only against the miners but against the working class of Great Britain and the whole world'.[104] A.J. Cook, the miners' leader, was similarly critical of the strike being called off without any guarantees.[105] Three points began to emerge in these criticisms: that the General Council betrayed the miners, which is debatable; that the TUC leadership was not committed to the struggle, which is correct; and that the strike was winnable, which was clearly incorrect. Conflated they imply that the General Strike was, in some way, a turning point in British trade union history.

Martin Jacques suggests the 'watershed' or 'turning point' thesis, a view that has also been supported by Alan Bullock and Patrick Renshaw.[106] The General Strike is seen as the last moment of a period of trade union militancy, after which the trade unions adopted a more cautious approach to strike action as their membership declined. These views do not accord with those of Gordon Phillips and Hugh Clegg, who maintain that the trajectory of trade union history did not change after 1926, that employers and trade unionists continued much as they had done before and that more peaceable industrial relations had been developing before 1926. Indeed, strike levels had been falling from the early 1920s and trade union membership did begin to increase from 1933 onwards, which throws doubt on 1926 being some type of major watershed.

Notwithstanding such an assessment it is clear that in the short run there were consequences. There was, for instance, a major debate throughout 1926 and 1927 during which the TUC attempted to stifle criticism of its actions and to produce its definitive explanation of the events leading to its calling, conducting and ending the General Strike. The General Council attempted to maintain a rule of silence, although there was some comment on the democratic nature of the trade union movement and general support for the miners at the TUC Conference at Bournemouth, 6–11 September 1926. Eventually it rebutted the various charges made against it at a Conference of Trade Union Executives on 20–21 January 1927.[107] Most particularly, it suggested that it had the full powers needed to make all the decisions in the dispute, that the miners effectively made consultation with them futile since they would not agree to negotiations, and that the government would have had to accept the Samuel Memorandum had the miners accepted it. Such suggestions are debatable, but the whole issue was less vitriolic than it might have been given that it took place within the context of government declaring its intention to take action to curb trade union power.

The Baldwin government had come to power in 1924 with the intention of tackling the political levy, the means by which trade unionists provided money for the Labour Party. The General Strike, the Astbury Judgment and the other events of May 1926 gave it, and the cabinet committee that was set up to produce legislation, further food for thought. However, the Trades Disputes and Trade Union Act, which came into force on 29 July 1927 was kaleidoscopic in the interests which it brought together, and lacked real direction and coherence. It contained eight main clauses, three of which prohibited sympathetic strike action, demanded that trade unionists should opt into paying the political levy, rather than opt out, and prevented some trade unions being connected with the TUC.

The impact of the 1927 Act was limited. It provoked only one or two cases in connection with sympathetic strike action before it was withdrawn in 1946, although it did reduce the number of trade unionists paying the levy for the Labour Party from 3,200,000 in 1927 to 2,000,000 in 1929.[108]

It is difficult to sustain the view that the General Strike was a turning point in British industrial relations, even though it had some short-term consequences for the trade union movement. The fact is that trade union membership was falling before the strike and continued to fall, at a slower rate, until the mid-1930s. The TUC lost some credibility but soon recovered, and the government was not able to effect any significant ban on sympathetic strike action.

Conclusion

The General Strike of 1926, the most important conflict in British industrial history, was the product of economic and social tensions of British society which saw the TUC attempting to defend the wages of its members at a time when the government was aiming to rationalise British industry and to reduce wage costs. The conflict could have occurred at any time but what determined that the action would take place in May 1926 was the conditions within the British coal industry.

The General Council of the TUC was reluctant to become too deeply involved in supporting the miners against wage cuts in 1925 and 1926 but, faced with the fact that it could not allow the trade union movement to let the miners down as it had done in April 1921, it was committed to a course of action which it did not believe in. It deluded itself into thinking that its action in calling a General Strike was simply industrial action to support the miners when in fact it was also a direct challenge to the government and the British Constitution. The government and the Communist Party saw what the implications of the TUC's sympathetic strike action were even if the TUC did not.

The government was well prepared for the strike, had created an administrative structure, turned Hyde Park into a food and milk centre and strategically positioned the armed forces in case of violence. Yet it soon realised that there was no revolutionary intent behind the actions of the General Council. It therefore waited for the General Council to call off the dispute, realising that without the approval of the miners the Samuel Memorandum would not provide the TUC with an escape route from conflict nor force the government to extend the coal mining subsidy.

The government's faith in the lack of commitment of the General Council was well founded. It organised the strike remarkably well, given the lateness of the preparations. Yet the local organisation was not important because the decision to call off the strike was taken at national, not local, level. It was an action which brought upon the General Council the criticism of the trade union movement and the Labour Left, but the damage was not permanent. Trade unions lost membership and the government introduced restrictive legislation, but by the early 1930s the trade union movement was advancing, not retreating, and the General Strike appears to have slowed down the attack of the employers on wages rather than speeded it up.

The General Strike may have been the subject of many marvellous myths but the reality is that it changed little. If anything, it revealed to the General Council the limits of the trade union movement and also encouraged it to seek more effective representation through the Labour Party. There had not been a General Strike of this type before and there has been none since. Never before, or since, was there such obvious social conflict within British society.

TUESDAY TO FRIDAY 27–30 APRIL

The events leading to the General Strike came to a climax in March and April 1926. The Samuel Commission reported on 10 March, suggesting wage reductions and a reorganisation of the coal industry. On 1 April the coal owners vaguely accepted the Samuel recommendations but insisted on district, rather than national, negotiations for wage rates and conditions of employment. The Miners' Federation of Great Britain refused to accept the idea of any wage reductions and regional negotiations on 13 April, and matters became more serious when, on 14 April, the mine owners issued lockout notices for 30 April, the day the government coal subsidy ended. With the end of the government subsidy it was clear that there was going to be serious industrial conflict which, in the light of the TUC's commitment to the miners, could lead to a general strike. The irony, of course, is that neither the government nor the TUC attempted to intervene directly until 25 April. At this point Arthur Pugh, chairman of the TUC, was invited to meet the prime minister at Chequers to discuss the coal crisis in an informal manner. The next day the prime minister met the Special Industrial Committee (SIC) of the General Council and asked it to appoint representatives to accompany the miners in any forthcoming discussions. The SIC in fact met the miners' leaders the same day. It was therefore almost two weeks after the battle lines had been drawn between the coal miners and the coal mine owners before the debate was widened to include the two most important organisations in the General Strike, the government and the TUC. Too little too late was the obvious conclusion to be drawn from the actions of both the government and the TUC as they suddenly awoke to the serious situation that faced them.

The government began to talk to both the Miners' Federation and the Mining Association on 27 April and Stanley Baldwin, the prime minister, gave the cabinet an account of the negotiations: 'The position was that the

Mineowners had at last agreed to enter an unfettered conference with the Miners, with the Prime Minister in the Chair. The negotiations were continuing and it was possible that he might find it necessary to ask the cabinet for decisions tomorrow.'[1] The resulting conference occurred on 28 April but led nowhere. Soon afterwards, at 7.15 p.m. on 30 April, the government was supporting the Organisation for the Maintenance of Supplies (OMS) circular which was asking volunteers to go to OMS offices.[2] The government also obtained from the coal owners a final offer of 20 instead of 33.3 per cent above the 1914 rates of pay, on condition that the working hours of miners would be extended from seven to eight hours per day. This change represented a smaller cut in pay and working standards but it was, nevertheless, a cut. This offer was clearly not going to be acceptable to the coal miners and, in any case, by this time, the coal owners' lockout was beginning to take effect.[3]

In the meantime the TUC had called a Special Conference of Trade Union Executives at Memorial Hall, Farringdon Street, London for Thursday 29 April. This was decided on 27 April when the TUC (SIC) and the miners also agreed in order to produce a declaration of policy which, once agreed by the General Council, became known as 'The Mining Situation'. This was laid before the trade union executives at the Special Conference, attended by more than 800 delegates on behalf of 141 trade unions affiliated to the TUC. The declaration argued that reorganisation was necessary for the coal industry. However, ignoring the TUC's concern that wage reductions might have to occur, it repeated the miners' policy that wages could not be reduced. Indeed, it stated that 'The wages and working conditions of mine workers are already so depressed as to render it imperative to seek for remedies other than a further degradation of the standard of life, or abrogation of the present standard hours. . . . The figures given in the [Samuel] Commission's Report show quite clearly that to seek any further degradation of this level [of wages] is indefensible.'[4]

With this policy before it the Special Conference spent the first day reviewing and responding to the seventeen main points of the Royal Commission on the Coal Industry (Samuel). It focused on the need to register the mine workers and to restrict recruitment into mining. Particular attention was paid to the responses of the miners to the sixteenth and seventeenth points.

16. NATIONAL NEGOTIATIONS We regard the maintenance of national negotiations an imperative, and the continuance of a National Wages Board.

17. Throughout the negotiations the Miners' Executive have repeatedly expressed their willingness to consider any proposal which the Government or the Mine Owners are prepared to submit for securing the speedy and effective reorganisation of the mining industry.[5]

After some discussion it was decided 'That this Conference endorsed the efforts of the General Council to secure an honourable settlement of the differences in the Coal Mining Industry. It further instructs the Industrial Committee of the General Council to continue further efforts and declare its readiness for the negotiations to continue, provided that [the coal owners' offer] is not enforced.'[6]

Soon afterwards, Ernest Bevin reminded the union delegates that 'In twenty-four hours from now you have to cease being separate unions. For this purpose you will have to become one union with no autonomy.'[7] Subsequently, there was a vote to give the General Council the responsibility for conducting the dispute and calling a strike if necessary. The SIC, which now became the Negotiating Committee, then took up the responsibility of settling the dispute and went to the House of Commons where it met Baldwin in the early hours of 30 April. He promised to contact the coal owners and to pass on their offer later in the morning. The harsh terms of the coal owners, already referred to, were received by the TUC and the miners at about 11.40 that morning and rejected by the miners.

There followed a number of feverish negotiations. At 2.20 p.m. the TUC (SIC) met the prime minister and asked for a withdrawal of the lockout notices in the mining industry. At 5.55 p.m. that day the Miners' Federation of Great Britain put forward a counter-proposal to the wage cuts, the last section of which read that 'until such [Samuel Report] re-organisation brought greater prosperity to the industry, the miners should not be called upon to surrender any of their present inadequate wages and conditions'. However, the prime minister felt that these proposals would run counter to those of the Samuel Commission.[8]

On the evening of 30 April, the miners' executive and the Negotiation Committee, along with Arthur Henderson and Ramsay MacDonald, further pressured Baldwin to get the lockout notices suspended. During a tetchy four to five-hour meeting, which involved four separate rounds of negotiations, Thomas produced a copy of an OMS poster (mentioned earlier) announcing the proclamation of a State of Emergency. The printers had refused to set it up at 7.15 p.m. According to Citrine:

> Jimmy Thomas looked the Prime Minister straight in the eye and asked him had this poster been ordered by the Government and did it represent the mind of the Government? Baldwin flushed and then, after a few seconds hesitation, said that it was true that the Government had taken the necessary steps to prepare for the proclamation of a state of emergency, but the poster had not yet been published. The silence was ominous. Every one of us concluded that we had been badly tricked.[9]

Although the government's action was natural, and on a par with the actions being undertaken by the TUC, trust evaporated immediately. At 8.45 p.m. the MFGB let it be known that it was not prepared for a reduction in wages as a preliminary to the reorganisation of the coal industry. At about 10 p.m. the TUC delegation to the prime minister returned to Memorial Hall, where Arthur Pugh gave a factual account of the day's proceedings. The general secretaries of the various unions were then taken to a room and each handed a copy of the 'Proposal for Co-ordinated Action'.[10] It stated that work would cease entirely in transport, printing, iron and steel, metal and heavy chemical industries at a time to be specified by the General Council. The builders were also to down tools on work other than hospitals. Yet health and sanitary arrangements were to be maintained and 'the Trade Unions concerned should do everything in their power to organise the distribution of milk and food to the whole population'. The concern of the document was to exert the maximum impact of the strike without causing danger and inconvenience to the public. Orderly activity was to be to the fore, with violence against property and riots to be avoided.

By the end of 30 April the scene was set for conflict. The miners and mine owners could not agree and the government and the TUC no longer trusted each other. The Samuel Commission recommendations still attracted the support of the TUC, perhaps rather more than the government which also espoused them, but seemed increasingly irrelevant as the forces of capital and labour came into conflict.

SATURDAY 1 MAY

On 1 May there were two major developments. The first was that the TUC meeting at Memorial Hall came to a conclusion with a ratification of the decision to support the miners with a general strike. The second was that Baldwin, and the Conservative government, decided to mount some last minute negotiations with the Negotiating Committee of the TUC while continuing to prepare for the emergency. The attempt to avoid conflict was now in its last throes.

It was the first event that was, perhaps, the most momentous moment in British industrial relations. J.H. Thomas had tried to keep his union, the National Union of Railwaymen (NUR), out of the dispute but was overruled by his executive and at 12.20 p.m. the historic endorsement of the General Strike began. The official report began with Arthur Pugh outlining the current situation, followed by the vote, Ernest Bevin discussing the arrangements, and the responses of both Herbert Smith, for the miners, and Ramsay MacDonald for the Labour Party.

Arthur Pugh, chair of Conference, announced to the delegates at 12.20 p.m. that:

> When we were before you last night it was to report with regret that we had been unable to induce the Government, or were unable to get the Government to induce the mine owners to respond to the request made by our Conference for a suspension of the notices in the mining industry to enable negotiations and discussions to proceed without having a threat hanging over our heads. We had to report to you that our mission in that respect had not been successful. Following that, the General Secretaries of the different Unions received a printed statement for a co-ordinated policy in relation to this dispute, to arrive at a definite decision with regard to the proposals contained in that scheme.[1]

Outside Memorial Hall, Farringdon Street, London, at the time of the fateful last meeting of the TUC before the beginning of the General Strike

By permission of the National Museum of Labour History

It was then proposed that the name of each union would be called out in alphabetical order and that the secretary or president of the particular union would indicate whether or not its executive committee had decided to adopt the proposal for co-ordinating activities and carrying on the dispute. Pugh added that,

> I want to make it clear that there are two important things involved in this scheme. The one relates specifically or more directly to our friends the Miners' Federation of Great Britain. The scheme requires that the Miners' Federation of Great Britain hand over to the General Council the conduct of this dispute. On that we have heard from the Miners' Federation through their President, Mr Smith, and their Secretary, Mr Cook, that that condition of the document is accepted by the Miners' Federation.

There was an adjournment and eventually a vote of 3,653,526 for and 49,911 against was announced, with trade unions representing 319,000 not being present. This vote prompted Ernest Bevin to discuss the organisation of the dispute with the meeting. Among other things, he stated:

Now, I am asked to call attention to the Memorandum and to say that you will readily realise that it is a hurried draft. Under circumstances when we had no thought of war, when I think that your General Council believed peace would accrue, and when you as a Conference decided on that very reasonable resolution the day before, we could not imagine – none of us can imagine – that any Government would have taken that document which was read to you and the subsequent discussions, but as offering a most admirable way to find peace and the reorganisation of this great industry. [Cheers] Now you will note on this document that we have deliberately determined to arrange for a volunteer service, notwithstanding that we are stopping vital services such as transport and the staple industries, we are prepared to arrange for, at least, the

The General Council of the TUC, 1926

By permission of the National Museum of Labour History

food of the people – and on behalf of the whole General Council, and I think in your name, it ought to go out that neither the Miners nor we have any quarrel with the people. [Cheers] We are not declaring war on the people. War has been declared by the Government, pushed on by sordid capitalism, and that being so we have said that there is no need for the OMS. We are prepared to distribute essential food stuffs. We offer to do it under a volunteer arrangement organised by the Trade Unions involved, and to see to it that the distribution, however long the struggle lasts, is an equitable one. I am also to state that arrangements as to who ought to be in and who ought to be out must not be raised. You must take your orders and obey them, believing that those of us charged with the responsibility of guiding will give the best guidance we can, and as to any of our members who are told to operate in a volunteer service in that way, it must be understood it is our declared policy and it must not be interfered with.

You will notice on the document that we have selected certain vital trades and staple trades to take the first brunt of the contest. Many more that are included in the first grade have responded magnificently in the affirmative. There must be no quibbling, now or when it is over. We look upon your 'Yes' as meaning that you have placed your all upon the altar for this great Movement, and having placed it there, even if every penny goes, if every asset goes, history will ultimately write up that it was a magnificent generation that was prepared to do it rather than see the miners down like slaves. [Cheers]

The last announcement I have to make – and this is a solemn one – is, that no person in the first grade must go to work at starting time on Tuesday morning; that is to say if a settlement has not been found. Those upon whom the call is made to take part in this struggle must refrain from working after the finish of shift on Monday night. . . .

Bevin was clearly concerned to make the strike effective, and yet not to make the TUC prone to the charge that it was directing its action at the public. It was a difficult tightrope to walk, since one could not have one without the other. The miners' leaders seemed highly pleased with developments. Herbert Smith (Miners' Federation) said to the conference that, 'I go away from London with no feeling of regret that we did not try to do everything possible to save the situation – the General Council and ourselves.' The Labour Party, represented by James Ramsay MacDonald MP, was less than sanguine in the matter and charged the Baldwin government with the collapse into industrial conflict.

> At ten o'clock last night, I confess to you, I believed that we had got peace, and to-day – and I ask the British public; not only you, but I ask the great mass of the people outside who do want justice done in this matter, who do believe in fair play, I ask them, irrespective of the twist that is given in the newspapers this morning, to believe what I say in that respect. And more, I ask them to read every word that Herbert Smith has said, and when they have done that, I will challenge them to come to any conclusion, but that the decision of the Government last night to break off negotiations was a crime against society. [Cheers] As Bevin has reminded us, it has been said, and it has been said with too much truth, that they who draw the sword will fall by the sword.
>
> My Friends and Colleagues, you can go away home this afternoon fully convinced that if the sword has been drawn, your representatives stood the last two days with their hands on the hilt of that sword, doing their best to prevent somebody else drawing that sword. And when it was drawn, towards midnight last night, it was not the hand of Thomas, not the hand of Herbert Smith, not the hand of any miner, not the hand of any man belonging to the General Council or to the Industrial Committee, it was the hand of the present Government that drew that sword and is now flaunting it in the face of the public of Great Britain.

Ramsay MacDonald's fine rhetoric, which swept over the precise facts of the situation, could barely hide the fact that what he was doing was what he had to do, as leader of the Labour Party, while obviously hoping that industrial conflict could be avoided.

The miners and the TUC leaders had come to an uneasy alliance. At their Federation Conference, on the evening of 30 April, the difficulties were outlined to the miners' representatives. A.J. Cook stated that, 'we felt all along the great danger of asking other people's help . . . they want to decide their position and that has meant a terrible struggle with your representatives'.[2] The fact was that by placing their emphasis on the reorganisation of the coal industry the TUC and the miners had managed to obscure the necessity of temporary wage cuts, which was an issue between them, and contained within the Samuel Report.

On the same day the General Council instructed the transport unions to establish local subcommittees that would be responsible for releasing foodstuffs and maintaining the health and sanitary provisions of the nation through a system of permits.[3] The statement of what they were to do was very vague and led to some confusion whereby both transport committees and local councils of action began to issue permits.

It remained, however, for Walter Citrine to inform the prime minister of the decision of the Special Conference. He wrote:

> I have to advise you that the Executive Committee of the Trades Union Congress including the Miners' Federation of Great Britain have decided to hand over to the General Council of the TUC the conduct of the dispute, and all negotiations in connection therewith will be undertaken by the General Council.
>
> I am directed to say that the General Council will hold themselves available at any moment should the Government desire to discuss the matter further.[4]

He sent another letter offering the services of the General Council in maintaining the essential services in the event of a stoppage.[5]

These letters prompted the prime minister to meet representatives of the Negotiating Committee of the TUC at 8.45 p.m., a meeting which was reduced to a smaller gathering at 11.00 p.m. with Baldwin, Lord Birkenhead, Steel-Maitland and Sir Horace Wilson in session with Pugh, Thomas, Swales and Citrine. At this meeting, Thomas stressed that the TUC representatives were bound by the resolution of the TUC which debarred them from negotiating without the withdrawal of lockout notices. Their main attention was thus directed at an attempt to extend the government subsidy to coal for two weeks so that a return to work could be secured. The two sections of the subcommittee sat in different rooms with Horace Wilson acting as intermediary. The TUC representatives seem to have developed some ill-founded confidence that the Samuel Report might yet form the basis of a settlement. Thomas favoured an acceptance of the report and felt that a settlement could be arranged within a fortnight. Other TUC negotiators clung to similar hopes. Indeed, in the early hours of Sunday morning a formula, devised by Sir Horace Wilson, was submitted to the TUC Negotiating Committee to the effect that 'The Prime Minister has satisfied himself as a result of conversations he had with the representatives of the Trades Union Congress, that if negotiations are continued (it being understood that the notices cease to be operative) the representatives of the Trades Union Congress are confident that a settlement can be reached on the lines of the [Samuel] Report within a fortnight.'[6] The meeting ended at about 1.15 a.m., 2 May with Pugh to contact his colleagues about developments.

In the meantime the government had introduced the Coal (Emergency) Directions, under the Emergency Powers Act, in order to control the stock of coal and to prevent hoarding. An extract from the directions issued by the County Borough of West Bromwich is reproduced below.

COUNTY BOROUGH OF WEST BROMWICH
NATIONAL EMERGENCY
SPECIAL ATTENTION of all people is drawn to the following
provisions of the
COAL (EMERGENCY) DIRECTIONS, 1926
RELATING TO
HOUSEHOLD OR DOMESTIC COAL

These directions are in force as from the 1 May 1926. Any person contravening the directions is guilty of a summary offence against the Emergency Regulations, 1926. Supplies of coal to dwelling houses are limited as follows:

Not lawful to buy more than 1 cwt in any one week.

Not lawful to buy any coal if already have more than 5 cwts.

Not lawful to sell to any person more than 1 cwt in any week.

Not lawful to sell to any person any coal if that person already has more than 5 cwts

COAL INCLUDES COKE

ALL PERSONS are earnestly requested to be as CAREFUL as they POSSIBLY CAN BE IN THE USE OF COAL, GAS AND ELECTRICITY.[7]

Developments on 1 May 1926 determined that the General Strike would almost certainly go ahead. The TUC leaders reluctantly accepted that they had to support the miners but still wished to gain a negotiated settlement. The government was similarly hopeful but was coming up with no solution that seemed more than a temporary measure. In the final analysis, both the government and the TUC seemed to be grasping at straws as the two directly involved combatants went their own way.

Catering for volunteers in Hyde Park. This group includes Mrs Causton (standing, left), Lady Mary Ashley Cooper and Lady Carmichael Anstruther seated, peeling potatoes, and Lady Quilter (standing, right)

By permission of the Illustrated London News *Picture Library*

SUNDAY 2 MAY

By 2 May both the government and the TUC were hardening their respective positions but still attempting to find a formula for settlement. Both bodies favoured an agreement based on the Samuel Report, but achieving such a settlement seemed increasingly unlikely.

The TUC soon fell into difficulty with the miners who were annoyed that it had met the government on the previous day and the morning of 2 May without their knowledge, the mining leaders having gone to the coalfields. At 1.15 p.m. A.J. Cook talked to the General Council and refused to accept the suggestions of a withdrawal of lockout and strike notices, the continuation of the subsidy for a fortnight and a settlement based on the Samuel Report. According to A.J. Cook, the miners' leaders were stung by the insouciant behaviour of the Negotiating Committee in meeting the government in secret 'in spite of their pledge to the miners only to negotiate with them'.[1] Nevertheless, the General Council persisted with this formula for a settlement and instructed the Negotiation Committee to find out more details of the government's intentions. Yet the miners would not be budged and at 4.30 p.m. Cook repeated the oft-quoted position of the miners: wage reductions were not on the agenda though they gave general support to the Samuel Report.[2]

On the other hand, the government wanted more detailed proposals than those being discussed. The cabinet, meeting at 12 noon on 2 May, declared: 'It was felt that negotiations involving the payment of a subsidy should not be renewed without a definite answer from the Miners in regard to their acceptance of the Report of the Royal Commission, which, of course, would commit the miners to make some sacrifice indicated in that Report. It was assumed that in any event the complete withdrawal of the threat of a general strike was *sine qua non* to any resumption of negotiations including a subsidy.'[3] The cabinet was also made aware of the fact that King George V had been informed of the situation.

During that afternoon, Baldwin and his ministers prepared an ultimatum for the TUC based on the miners' acceptance of adjustment to wages and hours and the unconditional withdrawal of the threat of a general strike prior to negotiations and reorganisation. This was in anticipation of what the cabinet agreed later at its resumed meeting at 9.30 p.m. The government had received no reply from the TUC by 9 p.m., for the miners' leaders had refused to discuss the new terms and had, temporarily, left London. Arthur Pugh and the TUC later met government representatives but noted that 'the lines of the Report' meant only a 'decline in wages'. Yet Pugh informed them that 'We will urge the Miners to authorise us to enter upon a discussion with the understanding that they and we accept the Report as a basis of settlement and we approach it with the knowledge that it may involve some reduction in wages.' This seemed to represent a shift of front from the previous evening when wage reductions were not going to be conceded by the TUC.[4]

The cabinet resumed its meeting and decided upon a statement, to be issued on 3 May:

> His Majesty's Government believed that no solution of the difficulties in the coal industry which is both practical and honourable to All concerned can be reached except by sincere acceptance of the Report of the Commission. . . .
>
> His Majesty's Government, therefore, before it can continue negotiations, must require from the Trade Union Committee both a repudiation of the actions referred to that have already taken place and an immediate and unconditional withdrawal of the instructions for a general strike.[5]

This statement influenced the government's discussions with the TUC, which meandered on that evening until the miners' executive arrived at Downing Street at 11.15 p.m. By that time the Wilson formula of the previous night, a settlement within two weeks based on the Samuel Report, was being floated again. Lord Birkenhead explained that this meant wage reductions and that the General Council would have to inform the miners of this. This was something which J.H. Thomas also accepted the need for. Yet the suggestion that the miners should be faced with the reality of the Samuel Report got nowhere. To avoid being bogged down, Ernest Bevin suggested that there should be an independent wages board which would be responsible for ensuring that reorganisation took place in advance of adjudicating wage rates. This board would recommend and approve the legislation necessary for reorganisation and the government, the miners and the mine owners would accept its decisions.[6] But this also did not get very far because of the cabinet ultimatum, already outlined, which effectively ended negotiations. The stark reality is that both the TUC and the government wanted some settlement based on the Samuel Report but could not get the miners to accept the wage reductions that it implied.

The discussions finally ended when the government realised that trade unions were sending telegrams to their members finalising strike arrangements. The imbroglio was ended in the early morning of 3 May by the refusal of the *Daily Mail* printers in London to set up the 'For King and Country' editorial on the threatened strike.

Although the government complained about the TUC and unions making arrangements it is clear that it had done the same. Most obviously J.C.C. Davidson, acting on behalf of Baldwin and operating through the Admiralty, had contacted the Newspaper Proprietors' Association on 1 May. He had met its representative, Lord Burnham, at 3.45 p.m. on Sunday 2 May at the Admiralty. Burnham indicated to him that his organisation favoured the government producing a news-sheet. The core of the idea of producing the *British Gazette* was born. Davidson recalled the resolutions of the Newspaper Proprietors' Association and the advice in his memoirs:

> 1st Resolution – That it is inadvisable to engage in joint publication of a newspaper during the present emergency and the members of this Association are not prepared to undertake such publication.

> 2nd Resolution – That in the event of the newspapers being suspended owing to a General Strike the members of this Association are of the opinion that it is advisable in the national interest that the Government should print daily bulletins giving essential news, and that such bulletins be displayed in Town Halls, Post Offices and other public buildings. It is suggested that the *London Gazette* might be an appropriate medium for this purpose.

3rd Resolution – That the members of this Association express their willingness to confer with the Government in carrying out this second resolution.

He [Burnham] stated that the London daily newspapers could not be issued after the following day (Monday); that the Bill Posters' Association had issued instructions to prevent any posting of Government Bills and announcements on public buildings and hoardings; and that the trade unions were introducing the Soviet system into all newspaper offices so that their agents could act as self-constituted censors and decide what to publish and what to suppress in the Labour interest. I asked him as to the best form of Government bulletin or news-sheet and he suggested that I, on behalf of the Government, should nominate somebody to act as official editor, while the editorial work should be carried out by experts supplied by the Newspaper Proprietors' Association. He said it was impossible to forecast the general attitude of the National Journalists. . . .[7]

By the end of 2 May there was little prospect that the General Strike would be avoided. Both the TUC and the government were clearing the decks for action and neither the miners nor the mine owners were in a mood for compromise. It soon became obvious that the Samuel Report was not going to be the basis of some national settlement. The miners would not accept the wage reductions that were implied in the report and the coal owners were reluctant to accept the reorganisation of the industry that would have been necessary.

Volunteers queuing outside the Foreign Office. They were offering to help in the maintenance of food supplies

By permission of the Illustrated London News *Picture Library*

MONDAY 3 MAY

The last opportunity to settle the impending strike disappeared early in the morning of 3 May when the government abandoned its meetings with the TUC because of the *Daily Mail* incident. Thereafter, both sides began to prepare for the forthcoming conflict which was scheduled to start at 11.59 p.m. on 3 May, and were deeply involved in a propaganda exercise to justify their position.

The *Daily Mail* incident is infamous in the folklore of labour history. It appears that the cabinet was already moving to end negotiations, as a result of pressure from its right wingers, when the news of the cessation of work at the *Daily Mail* came through. In the early morning of 3 May between 12.45 and 1.15 a.m., Pugh, Thomas, Swales and Citrine were called out of discussions between the General Council and the miners' leaders to meet Baldwin who handed them a note which referred to 'overt acts . . . including interference with the freedom of the Press' as grounds for ending the talks between the government and the TUC. They later referred to the fact that they 'were entirely without responsibility for the "overt acts" referred to' but were told that Baldwin had retired for the night.[1] The TUC representatives went next door to their colleagues and then to their colleagues at Eccleston Square. There they prepared a reply disowning the printers' strike and deploring the curtailment of negotiations. They also formed a subcommittee of Bevin, Pugh, Citrine, Smith, Richardson and Cook, to complete the outline agreements which were being discussed when the government called an end to negotiations. Later that day the TUC and the miners agreed to a statement about the need to reorganise the coal industry through a wages board and then to discuss wages. In other words, reorganisation was to come before any wage reduction and the Samuel Report was being rearranged.

The irony of this abrupt end to negotiations is that although NATSOPA members refused to set up the leader article entitled 'For King and Country' for the *Daily Mail*, it was in fact printed in the

Manchester edition. The passage that the printers objected to ran as follows: 'A General Strike is not an industrial dispute. It is a revolutionary movement which can only succeed by destroying the Government and subverting the right and liberties of the people.'[2]

There was in fact a last-minute attempt to resolve the dispute when Ernest Bevin contacted Horace Wilson at about 5 p.m. with new proposals. There was a possibility that they would be raised in the House of Commons by Ramsay MacDonald, but this did not occur. Ramsay MacDonald and Arthur Henderson did meet Baldwin, Chamberlain, Churchill and Steel-Maitland at 10 p.m. Nothing came of this initiative since the government ministers had already declared that they would not take action until the withdrawal of the strike notices.[3]

Faced with a strike within hours, the TUC quickly issued a manifesto to explain its position in the whole affair. It stated that:

> The General Council, with the full approval and cooperation of the accredited representatives of the trade unions has been compelled to organize united resistance to the attempt to enforce a settlement of the mining problem at the expense of the mine-workers' wages. At a special conference of trade union executives on Thursday, Friday and Saturday last measures were taken by the General Council to bring about a stoppage of work in the transport services, the printing trade, and certain productive industries. Unless a settlement, which the representatives of the Trades Union Congress can recommend the miners accept, is reached before midnight on Monday the workers in these essential industries and services will be withdrawn.
>
> The trade unions disclaim all responsibility for the calamity that now threatens. Their action is not directed at the public. Responsibility for the consequences that must inevitably follow a general cessation of work lies with the mine-owners and the Government entirely.[4]

The TUC was clearly aware that the public would be inconvenienced by the General Strike and that the government would use this to increase the hostility towards the trade unions. It was most sensitive to its weak and confused position, wishing to settle but being thwarted by the miners' leaders insistence that wages would not be reduced.

Yet it was the government that seized the initiative. Both Stanley Baldwin, the prime minister, and Winston Churchill spoke to the House of Commons later that day. Baldwin outlined the events of the previous few days stressing that, 'if we could have got that complete assurance [of a settlement based upon the Samuel Report], we would have risked it; we would have asked for another fortnight, and, I think, we would have paid for another fortnight. But it was no good going on, with the experience we had for the past fortnight, in any negotiations unless we could have some assurance that there was a reasonable hope of success.'[5] It was with this hope in mind that the Conservative government pursued its attempts to bring about a resolution of the developing conflict. Yet Baldwin argued that such hopes were dashed when the TUC 'secured on Saturday last plenary powers to order a strike without notice. This was done, I imagine, without prior consultation with, or authority from, their members and branches . . . . I do not believe that there was anything like a thorough-going consultation with the rank and file before this despotic power was put into the hands of a small executive power in London.'

To the government, the problem seemed to be that the trade union leaders, most of whom wanted peace, were unaware of the pressures they had released.

> Perhaps they thought that there was nothing more at stake than bringing a certain amount of spectacular pressure to bear which might suffice to persuade the Government to capitulate without serious damage to the liberties of the nation, but *they have created a machine which they cannot control*. I tried to co-operate with Mr Pugh and his colleagues in the search for an agreement to the last possible moment, but I *became convinced last night (Sunday) that Mr Pugh and those with him were not in control of the situation*, and that it would be wrong and dangerous for the Government to continue talking unless we got an immediate and unconditional withdrawal of the instructions for the general strike.

Baldwin was in fact correct in his assessment. He then took the offensive and suggested that the General Strike imperilled the 'freedom of our very Constitution'. Winston Churchill, in an aggressive supporting speech, accused the TUC of attempting to overthrow the government, emphasised

Baldwin's points and suggested that there was an open door for the General Council if they 'withdrew the challenge they have issued'.

Labour MPs responded to the government assault in an attempt to temper the impression that the trade unions were challenging the Constitution. Ramsay MacDonald said that 'I am putting the case at which, at twenty minutes past seven on Monday, the man who stands for peace takes his stand; and I am going for peace at twenty minutes past seven on Tuesday and Wednesday, and right through until it is finished.' J.H. Thomas also asked, 'Is it too late? I do not believe it is too late to avert what I believe is the greatest calamity to this country', adding that 'the responsibility of trying to save it all rests upon us'.

The Commons debate of 3 May was, indeed, an interesting indication of how the three major political parties viewed the General Strike. On the one hand, Thomas, representing the TUC and Labour Party line, abhorred a general strike which challenged the Constitution and emphasised that the impending dispute was something that says 'We don't want to overthrow everything. It is merely a plain, economic, industrial dispute where the workers say we want justice.'⁶ At the other extreme, there was the attitude of the Conservative Party, as expressed by Winston Churchill, which saw the General Strike as a challenge to the Constitution. Between the two extremes lay David Lloyd George, the effective leader of the Liberal Party, who saw the General Strike as a mistake since it was designed to get the government to take action and did not arise from an ordinary dispute. Yet, equally, he felt that it was 'a very serious mistake' for the government to announce that it would not negotiate under duress. Most Liberals would have agreed with David Lloyd George, the exception being Sir John Simon who later took the government line. Opinion was quite clearly divided but there is no doubt that the government had won the debate.

It now undertook immediate preparations for the dispute. The Emergency Powers Act, which allowed the government to requisition food, fuel, stores, vehicles and tramways, was now in place. It also allowed the police to act without a warrant, and meetings could be prohibited. Churchill and J.C.C. Davidson also met the representatives of the Newspaper Proprietors' Association at 12 noon and were offered the facilities of the *Morning Post* to produce a government publication. At 9.45 p.m. Churchill called a meeting in his room in the House of

Commons at which it was decided to use the offices of the *Morning Post* and to produce a newspaper, under the auspices of HMSO, to be called the *British Gazette*. Later that day, Davidson met Baldwin to discuss the situation; the former subsequently wrote that:

> When Baldwin and I were talking over things, he said to me, 'Why don't you give Winston the *British Gazette*?' I said, 'Well, so far as I can I will.' He said 'Well, it will keep him busy, stop him doing worse things', to which I agreed. He then said 'I'm terrified of what Winston is going to be like', and I said, 'So am I, but I've got my terms of reference, my instructions, and my position, and so long as I'm supported as being the executive head I don't care a damn what Winston says; he's got no power except the power of personality which is very difficult to deal with, but he has no executive power and I propose to censor. If Winston tries to turn the men into an army of Bolsheviks . . . I shall resist that. SB said 'That's absolutely right, of course you will.' Therefore some conflict with WS [Churchill] but he bore no ill will.[7]

Churchill did edit the *British Gazette* and Davidson did censor him.

In addition to deciding to run a newspaper the government arranged to broadcast news bulletins five times a day – at 10 a.m., 1 p.m., 4 p.m., 7 p.m. and 10 p.m. – and to produce three government pamphlets for distribution during the strike. Put immediately to work the Wireless Broadcast Messages quoted a passage from the prime minister's statement in the House of Commons to the effect that, 'There will never be any settlement in the Coal Industry until there is a different spirit in it and a very different organisation for the settlement of wages. Owners and miners must find some way, or have some way found for them, of settling their differences without Government intervention, as in the case of other big industries.'[8]

More immediately, a temporary hutment was set up in the Foreign Office quadrangle; men and students had been registering for voluntary work at a rate of about 400 per hour. Hyde Park was also closed to the public, a complete telephone network was set up in the park and many temporary huts and buildings were being erected.

The trade unions also began to make their own preparations in earnest. Those unions representing the front line workers, who would be answering the immediate call for strike action, contacted their employers' organisations. For instance, C.T. Cramp, of the National Union of Railwaymen, wrote a standard letter to all the main railway companies, including the one below to Sir Felix J.C. Pole, general manager of the Great Western Railway, based at Paddington. He explained:

Miners' Crisis

Arising out of the dispute in the Coal Industry this Union in common with others affiliated to the Trades Union Congress has agreed to give its support to the Miners during the present lockout and further, in accordance with the decision arrived at, at a Conference of Trade Union Executives covered by the General Council of the Trades Union Congress, it has been agreed to take steps in conjunction with the Transport Workers' Unions, to call upon our members to cease work on Monday next, the instant.

I am conveying this intention to you in order that you may be cognisant of the fact that in ceasing work the men are acting upon the instructions of the National Union of Railwaymen. . . .[9]

Pole's response was to issue a notice to all staff warning them to 'hesitate before you break your contract of service with the old Company, before you inflict injury upon the railway Industry, and before you arouse ill-feeling in the railway Service which will take years to remove'.[10]

This shadow-boxing of threat and counter-threat pervaded the activities of 3 May as both sides marshalled their forces and arguments for the coming industrial conflict. The government was determined to win the propaganda war and the minds of the British public while the TUC and the Labour Party, with some reluctance and protestation of innocent involvement, attempted to ensure an honourable performance on behalf of the miners even if they did believe that the Samuel Report, with its implications for wages, was the only way forward. As for Sir Herbert Samuel, the man whose report was at the centre of the debate – he was on holiday at San Vigilio in the Italian lakes. However, he telegraphed Baldwin to offer his services as a negotiator. It is indicative of the attitude of the government that his offer was rejected. None the less, he decided to return to Britain in order to see what help he could give.

TUESDAY 4 MAY

The first full day of the General Strike began with an eerie silence at the railway stations, with the London Underground at a virtual standstill, and bus and transport services throughout the rest of the country almost totally abandoned. The vast majority of workers in the vital industries had heeded the call of the General Council and their own unions and had not turned up for work. Indeed, it is estimated that between 1.5 million and 1.75 million workers came out on strike in support of the 1 million or so locked-out miners. They included workers employed in transport, printing, iron and steel, power stations, building and the chemical industries. A.J. Cook, the miners' leader, wrote later that 'Tuesday, May 4th, started with the workers answering the call. What a wonderful response! What loyalty! What solidarity! From John O'Groats to Land's End the workers answered the call to arms to defend us, to defend the brave miner in his fight for a living wage.'[1] The TUC was similarly effusive at a special press conference held at Eccleston Square in announcing that 'Reports from Land's End to John O'Groats have surpassed all our expectations . . . not only the railwaymen and transport workers, but those in other trades have come out in a manner we did not quite expect immediately. The General Council's difficulty has been to keep men at work in the trades that are in the second line of defence.'[2] Yet the government was, at the same time, playing down the sense of alarm and suggesting that food supplies were normal and that it was in control of the situation. The irony of this is that both sides were relatively effective within their own spheres as the strike continued. The TUC could claim to have brought transport to a halt while the government could maintain that it still had civil control and was able to ensure adequate food supplies. Yet the first full day of the General Strike was characterised by a sense of hiatus, some minor disturbances and propaganda exercises.

The streets of London were packed with people walking to work and the roads were blocked with cars. There were some very nasty moments, mainly at the Blackwall Tunnel with crowds of strikers stopping cars and making passengers get out and walk. The police had to make baton charges and the casualties were taken to Poplar Hospital. There were also disturbances in Canning Town in east London where crowds were also stopping cars and even smashing engines. The London docks were also closed and subject to intense picketing. In most other urban centres there were no corporation trams and buses. In Sheffield, the great iron, steel and engineering firms, such as Hatfields, Cammell Lairds and Vickers, were closed or just ticking over. *The Times* appeared as a four, rather than a twenty-four, page paper.

The government and pro-government forces were quick to prepare for action. The government ordered 450 tons of newsprint by telephone from Holland to come into the Pool of London, since there was only ten days' supply of paper available in Britain. Messrs Bowater's mill at Northfleet was commandeered to store it and about 200 volunteers were gathered from various sources to work on the paper-making machines.[3] The Wireless Broadcast Messages informed the public that some 500 lorries for the transport of food in London had assembled by the morning, that there were large numbers of volunteers for service available in London and all over the country and that no less than 6,000 volunteers had enrolled at the Foreign Office up to 7 p.m. on the previous night.[4] The general manager's report of the Great Western Railway indicated that 1,416 volunteers enrolled at Paddington, of whom 367 were quickly employed, and that 637 men had enrolled as special constables.[5] Naval ratings were unloading a cargo of tomatoes from the Channel Islands at Weymouth, and 48 dining car men had reported for duty at Paddington and were being asked to volunteer for essential services.[6]

The TUC, on the other hand, was still undecided as to what action to take. What is often not realised is that the TUC did not take immediate control of the dispute. Although the General Council was responsible for the negotiations and the conduct of the dispute, it had in fact left the individual trade unions to take the necessary action. On 4 May Ernest Bevin suggested to the General Council that he should take supreme control of the organisation of the strike. His ideas were rejected, although they were soon to become a necessity.[7] Indeed, the confusion that was arising from not having one person in control was evident in the comments of Councillor W. Mellor, secretary of Manchester Trades and Labour Council: 'I anticipate we shall act as the food distributor under the voluntary system agreed upon by the trade unions, *but we have no definite instructions to point to yet.* It may be that the railway workers and the transport workers will carry out the distribution under their own direction.'[8]

It was at this point that there was also pressure for the TUC to produce its own newspaper. On the evening of 3 May the Printing and Kindred Trades Federation suggested to the Publishing Committee of the TUC that the *Daily Herald* be allowed to continue production. This appeal was rejected but Hamilton Fyfe, the editor of the *Daily Herald*, met the committee on 4 May to suggest that the TUC needed a paper since the government was about to publish its own. It was decided that the TUC would publish a paper, the *British Worker*, at the price of a penny, from 5 May. However, there was the immediate problem that many printers at the *Herald* were concerned that to work on such a paper would be to break the spirit of the strike. Indeed, Fyfe could only induce the *Herald* printers to work on the night of 4 May with the help of a written authorisation from the General Council.[9]

Even before the government or the TUC had got their propaganda machinery into gear, the Fascists, despite being a very small group, were producing their own propaganda newspaper against the strike. The National Fascisti came out in favour of the government with a strongly racialist attack on S. Saklatvala, who was of Indian origin. Suggesting that Battersea had been taken over by the Bolsheviks it noted that there was a 'warrant out for our one and only coloured MP', in connection with a speech he had made in Hyde Park on May Day. They printed an 'Open Letter No. 1 to Parsee Pawnee-Wallah (Very Temporary) MP for N/B, London'. The extract below reveals the extent of the racialist abuse that was being levelled at Saklatvala:

> You are supposed to be an 'Honourable' Member of the House of Commons, a place which you should consider it an honour to enter, but apparently do not. In that House you have recently made a speech full of what the true Briton – whatever his faults may be – Winston Churchill, has termed 'terminological inexactitudes', but what the 'man in the street' plainly calls LIES.

In that speech you stated that of the 400,000,000 people which yourself admit composed the British Empire not less than 340,000,000 of these (and of which of course you are one) 'have no traditional sentiment in regard to the Union Jack'. This is untrue. . . .

Amongst the 339,999,999 (plus one Parsee) who have no 'traditional sentiment' I presume that you include the too large number of 'coloured persons' like yourself, brought from a condition of filth, slavery, savagery, and ignorance by the efforts of a brave and loyal handful of Britons who do possess 'traditional sentiments' and who have been suborned and seduced from a rightful loyalty to Britain by such glib-tongued sedition mongers as you.

You may jeer at fascism, Oh Parsee Pawnee-Wallah, but Fascism will live long after Communism is but a forgotten shibboleth; long after even Conservatism, Socialism, Liberalism and Internationalism lie 'perdu' midst the dusty tomes of 'Hansard'. Communism is wrong, and you know it, Parsee. We the National Fascisti of Great Britain, and the Empire Overseas, know full well that you are but an Adventurer, sitting on the Raft of Opportunity, afloat on the Red Sea of Communism, eagerly awaiting the Wind of Revolution . . . .

The President, The National Fascisti[10]

The outpourings and activities of the Fascists, of course, added little to the dispute. The Fascists were, in fact, far too insignificant for that, and very few people would have had access to their publications even in the West End of London where they began to distribute their literature. It was only grist to the mill of the nationalism that pervaded the thinking of the Right in the burgeoning industrial conflict.

Far more significant was the help provided by undergraduates from Oxford, Cambridge and other universities. About 460 Cambridge undergraduates, the 'plus-four brigade', volunteered to work in the docks. One of these was Henry Duckworth, who became one of the chief organisers of the 'Dover Dockers', better known as the 'Dover Fifty', who acted as strike-breakers throughout the dispute. On 4 May, having failed to organise all the Trinity College men into a volunteer force, he decided to organise 'all the fittest and ablest in Cambridge' to volunteer for the docks.[11] Thousands of other undergraduates also began to volunteer for the docks, the railways and other forms of voluntary work.

The first full day of the General Strike lacked any major initiatives – it was too early for that – or any particular dramatic events beyond the fact that the nation's transport came to a halt. Both sides were attempting to assess the impact of the dispute and, apart from the process of registering volunteers and crowds of strikers stopping the movement of cars in some areas, relatively little happened.

University students unloading vessels at Hay's Wharf, London Bridge

By permission of the Illustrated London News *Picture Library*

WEDNESDAY 5 MAY

On 5 May both sides in the dispute began to assess their respective positions, to develop their propaganda machines and to claim significant successes. The most important of these developments was that the TUC began to improve its organisation. It also produced its *British Worker* based on the *Daily Herald* and its editor Hamilton Fyfe, while the government produced its much-vaunted *British Gazette*, with Winston Churchill as editor and J.C.C. Davidson as censor.

Of most immediate importance to the TUC was its decision to assume much more control of the strike through the Powers and Orders Committee which was renamed the Strike Organisation Committee (SOC). This committee, which covered all aspects of the strike including food and public services, was dominated by Ernest Bevin and Alfred Purcell (the chairman). Although theoretically it reported to the General Council it in fact issued orders on its own account. It ran the strike in a direct form from 5 to 7 May, but became more concerned with negotiating a settlement from then onwards.[1]

The first edition of the *British Gazette*, of which 232,000 copies were printed, also appeared on 5 May. It was a breezy attempt to suggest that the government was in control. It reported on the way in which city gents were going to Mill Hill Gas Works to keep the boilers stocked with coal and how at other London power stations naval ratings were keeping the fires well stoked. It, and some provincial newspapers, reported on the attempts to get the transport services working again. The London General Omnibus Company, which had run no trams on the first day of the strike, had eighty-six operating on 5 May, and was in fact providing a 7½ minute service.[2] There were also attempts in most towns and cities to get some makeshift tram system operating. In Leeds, the first trams left Boar Lane and Briggate and went to Headingley and Dewsbury Road but, even with police travelling on the trams, nine had their windows broken.[3] There were about forty provincial newspapers produced throughout the country, despite the strike, and the British Fascisti continued to produce their paper and to distribute it in both the East End and West End of London.

From the *British Gazette* and the right-wing press it would appear that the armed forces were keeping a relatively low profile. Nevertheless, the navy was showing the flag with two big warships moored in the Clyde, with the light cruiser *Comus* sent to Glasgow, two destroyers to Newcastle, and in Liverpool the warships HMS *Barham* and *Ramillies* along with HMS *Derry* and smaller craft being moored to allow their crews to unload some of the ships diverted from the London docks. In London submarines moored in the docks were supplying electricity for refrigerated warehouses. In effect, every major port had a naval presence. Bluejackets with fixed bayonets were being brought into other industrial areas, soldiers were working at the side of volunteer drivers at Chiswick bus depot. All army leave was stopped and there were troop movements. A battalion of the Somerset Regiment had been sent to Cardiff, a battalion of the South

A submarine being used in the London docks to provide an electricity supply for refrigerated warehouses

By permission of the TUC

Army tank with troops from the Wellington Barracks, London
By permission of the National Museum of Labour History

Wales Borderers to Liverpool and other detachments from Aldershot to Catterick and Carlisle for possible use in Scotland. The Wellington Barracks in London, with its tanks, was to become the focus of much activity. At this stage both Churchill and Lord Birkenhead, the cabinet hawks, were discussing the need to use the troops to break the heavy picketing occurring at the London docks, although without much success.

The government did, however, move in other ways to reduce the effectiveness of the strike. The Ministry of Health issued Circular 703 to instruct Boards of Guardians running the Poor Law not to provide relief for the strikers. The gist of it is presented here:

> The function of the Guardians is the relief of destitution within the limits prescribed by law and they are in no way concerned in the merits of an individual dispute, even though it results in application for relief. They cannot, therefore, properly give any weight to their views of such merits in dealing with the application to be made.
>
> The question for consideration of the Guardians on any application for relief made by a person who is destitute in

consequence of a trade dispute or questions of fact, namely, whether the applicant for relief is or is not a person who is able-bodied and physically capable of work; whether work is or is not available for him and if such work is not available for him, whether it is or is not so unavailable through his own act or consent.

Where the applicant for relief is able-bodied and physically capable of work the grant of relief to him is unlawful if work is available to him or he is thrown on the Guardians through his own act or consent.[4]

This was a clear statement that those involved in the General Strike could not be given relief in their own right, although, of course, their dependants could receive some relief. It is quite clear that this was designed to stop some Boards of Guardians, dominated by the Labour

George Lansbury (left), Labour leader and newspaper editor, and Hamilton Fyfe, editor of the *Daily Herald* and the *British Worker*

By permission of the TUC

Special constables being briefed and given staves and armbands

By permission of the National Museum of Labour History

Party, supporting the strike through Poor Law relief. It was most decidedly aimed at some guardians in Poplar and South Wales.

The government also declared, as already hinted at, its intent to raise the number of special constables in London to 50,000 and to set up a Civil Constabulary Reserve, drawn mainly from the Territorial Army and former soldiers. In addition, about 200,000 'second' reserve policemen were mobilised throughout England and Wales, outside London. In addition by 5 May the government had between 300,000 and 500,000 volunteers at its disposal and most of its districts had 20,000 or more volunteers. In fact, most of these were never to be used in the conflict.[5]

The fact is that there had not been the great breakdown of authority which the government feared. Nevertheless, in one major respect the authorities and the private companies could do little. The railways had

Special constables being trained to tackle the enemy

By permission of the National Museum of Labour History

been effectively brought to a halt by the strike of NUR and ASLEF members. The welter of statistics available suggests that most railway companies were running less than 1 per cent of their freight volume and that passenger volume varied between 3.7 and 5.1 per cent.[6]

The most controversial aspect of the government's activities on 5 May was the fact that the *British Gazette* mounted a strong attack on the trade union movement. This produced heated exchanges in the House of Commons. J.R. Clynes described the government newspaper as a scandalous publication, and Labour MPs reiterated the point. The home secretary, Sir William Joynson-Hicks, said that the government took full responsibility for the matter produced in the *Gazette*, but then demanded notice of the question when a Labour MP asked if he had seen the notice attacking the unions, and whether it was the function of the government to publish such propaganda.[7] The whole proceedings were watched by

Herbert Smith and A.J. Cook who were in the Strangers' Gallery, along with the Prince of Wales. The home secretary also noted that 11,000 constables had been enrolled in London and that more were needed, subsequently making an appeal for more through the BBC. Before this altercation in the House of Commons, the prime minister had informed his colleagues that the letter of 1 May from the TUC General Council offering to enter arrangements for the distribution of essential foodstuffs 'had not been and would not be answered'.[8] The prime minister later announced to the House of Commons that, 'No Government in any circumstances could ever yield to a general strike. The moment it was called off unconditionally the Government were prepared to resume negotiations.'[9]

The TUC also produced its first issue of the *British Worker* which focused on two themes – the amazing response of the workers and the intimidation of some students to persuade them to join the OMS. On the first point the following report was produced by the General Council.

WONDERFUL RESPONSE TO THE CALL
GENERAL COUNCIL'S MESSAGE STAND FIRM AND KEEP OUT

The workers' response has exceeded all expectations. The first day of the great General Strike is over. They have manifested their determination and unity to the whole world. They have resolved that the attempt of the mine owners to drive three million men, women and children into starvation shall not succeed.

All the essential industries and all the transport services have been brought to a standstill. The only exception is that the distribution of milk and food has been permitted to continue. The Trades Union Congress is not making war on the people. It is anxious that the ordinary members of the public shall not be penalised for the unpatriotic conduct of the mineowners and the Government.

Never have the workers responded with greater enthusiasm to the call of their leaders. The only difficulty that the General Council is experiencing, in fact, is in persuading those workers in the second line of defence to continue at work until the withdrawal of their labour may be needed.

WORKERS' QUIET DIGNITY

The conduct of the trade unionists, too, constitutes a credit to the whole movement. Despite the presence of armed police and the military, the workers have preserved a quiet orderliness and dignity, which the General Council urges them to maintain, even in the face of the temptation and provocation which the Government is placing in their path.

To the unemployed, also, the General Council would address an earnest appeal. In the present fight there are two sides only – the workers on the one hand and those who are against them on the other.

Every unemployed man or woman who 'blacklegs' on any job offered by employers or the authorities is merely helping to bring down the standard of living for the workers as a whole, and to create a resultant situation in which the number of unemployed is greater than ever.

The General Council is confident that the unemployed will realise how closely their interests are involved in a successful issue to the greatest battle ever fought by the workers of the country in the defence of the right to live by work.

In other words, the TUC was emphasising the respectable and orderly nature of the conflict and attempting to draw into it the support of the unemployed. Its whole emphasis was placed on the need to defend the wages and the standard of living of the whole working class. It was a message that was repeated in many local strike bulletins, some of which also reproduced the official TUC statement which noted the amazing response of the workers from Land's End to John O'Groats.[10]

The second point was that the first issue of the *British Worker* was concerned about an interview with a student at University College, London, who wished to 'expose the mean methods employed to induce students to enrol in the OMS and fight the workers'. The gist of the interview was that in the previous couple of days the provost, Sir Gregory Foster, and the college secretary, Dr W. Seton, who was a founder member of the OMS, had held meetings with students. One meeting had begun with a declaration of its non-political nature, but they made an appeal to the students to support the Government, and finally insisted on the necessity of everyone immediately joining the OMS.

As a bait to loyal students their services would be remembered and taken into consideration during the examinations. This promise drew many recruits, a great many of whom feared victimisation by university authorities if they failed to enrol in support of the Government.

It was decided that the issue would be raised by Labour MPs in the House of Commons but it was lost sight of as more important issues began to develop over the next few days.

The *British Worker* was designed to maintain the morale of the strikers, to rebut the charges of the government and to publish the instructions of the TUC. Its prospects of achieving these objectives looked slim on 5 May when there was a police raid on the offices of the *Daily Herald*, where it was produced. However, despite the inconvenience, the government allowed the *British Worker* to be published.[11]

The second full day of the General Strike had thus seen the further development of the propaganda war between the government and the TUC, in which both sides claimed victory. The real issues of the General Strike – of its legality, control of food movements and possible settlement – had not been addressed and, like the first full day, there was a hiatus in which little more than shadow boxing occurred.

THURSDAY 6 MAY

Thursday 6 May saw a change of atmosphere in the dispute. There were violent, although relatively minor, disturbances, the government began to emphasise the threat to the authority of constitutional government and the TUC began to look for a swift and peaceful settlement to the dispute under the auspices of Sir Herbert Samuel. Perhaps the most vital event was the government attack on the unconstitutional nature of the strike, which was supported by Sir John Simon, a prominent Liberal MP. The government was clearly becoming more confident and determined as the dispute wore on while the TUC General Council was appearing less resolute as it initiated peace talks.

From the outset of the dispute the government had decided that the BBC radio would be one of its major propaganda weapons, aiming at the two million or so people who had licences for crystal sets. This contrasted with the view of John Reith, director-general of the BBC, who wished to provide a reliable news service that was impartial, although he soon recognised that the situation was unusual. Reith wrote to Davidson on 6 May making the point that 'this is not a time for dope', but arguing that a reliable news service 'might improve appreciation of the fact that a prolongation of the stoppage is a sure means of reducing wages and the standard of living, which it is the avowed intention of trade unionists to improve. . . .'[1] Complete impartiality was out of the question but Reith felt that the BBC should try to preserve its reputation for accuracy and fair play. In fact he was never given the opportunity to operate in this manner, for the threat was that the government would take over control of the BBC if Reith attempted to broadcast impartially. This obviously explains why the BBC only permitted government ministers and representatives to transmit one viewpoint to the nation.

Baldwin also took the dispute to the TUC by issuing a message to the nation. In it he stated that:

Strikers stopping a blackleg van

By permission of the National Museum of Labour History

A bus destroyed in the East End of London

By permission of the National Museum of Labour History

Constitutional Government is being attacked. Let all good citizens whose livelihood and labour have thus been put in peril bear with fortitude and patience the hardship with which they have been so suddenly confronted. Stand behind the Government, who are doing their part, confident that you will co-operate in the measures they have undertaken to preserve the liberties and privileges of the people of these islands. The laws of England are the people's birthright. The laws are in your keeping. You have made Parliament their guardian. The General Strike is a challenge to Parliament and is the road to anarchy and ruin.[2]

It was the last sentence which was most often repeated in the various

The fate of a strike-breaking car

By permission of the National Museum of Labour History

provincial newspapers as well as in the *British Gazette*, whose circulation had by this time increased to 507,000.

The message was driven home in the House of Commons late that evening. There were general mutterings in the House about the legality of the dispute and at 11.15 p.m. Sir John Simon stood up to make a speech. The gist of what he said was that most strike action was legal, 'But once people proclaimed a general strike they were, as a matter of fact, starting a movement of a perfectly different and wholly unconstitutional character. [Labour laughter] A strike was a strike against employers to compel employers to do something. A general strike was a strike against the General Public to make the Public, Parliament and Government do something.'[3]

Most Labour MPs had withdrawn before Simon made his speech and there were only three members left in the House of Commons. One of these, Duncan Graham, called the speech hypocritical while another, George Lansbury, made an emotional point about the problems of the poor.[4]

These criticisms from Baldwin and Simon operated within the context of the rising level of violence that was occurring. There were trivial, but ugly, violent scenes at the Elephant and Castle route centre in south London. The mounted police were much in evidence as the milling crowds attempted to interfere with the transport. There was a police charge on strikers in Tooley Street, Southwark, that led to thirty-two arrests.[5] In Poplar the police faced jeering strikers. Indeed, incidents like this in London produced the first fatality of the strike when a bus driven by volunteers was forced into the pavement by a threatening crowd. The bus hit a man who died soon afterwards. There was news too of violence in Middlesbrough, in the eastern suburbs of Glasgow, in Edinburgh and in Aberdeen. The Aberdeen disturbances came as a result of the decision of the town council to restart the bus service. The crowd attacked the first bus down Belmost Street and the volunteers, mainly students, were molested.[6] By the afternoon the police had assembled in force at the corner of Union Street and Belmost Street and also at the Queen's Cross depot. Coal was thrown at a bus, lorries had their windows smashed and there were baton charges by the police.

At Middlesbrough there were ugly scenes in the evening as a crowd of about 4,000 prevented the level crossing gates from being closed and tried

Wiring up buses to protect them from angry strikers

By permission of the National Museum of Labour History

to wreck a train by chaining lorries as obstacles to the rails. The crowd then invaded Middlesbrough station and did considerable damage, as well as badly injuring Mr Walker, the stationmaster, with a thrown stone. The police beat off the crowd with truncheons and the mayor appealed for them to disperse, only narrowly escaping injury from a flying bottle.

The authorities and the government were spurred into action and the local police forces made numerous arrests. The Indian Communist MP for Battersea North, Shapurji Saklatvala, was sentenced to two months' imprisonment for his inflammatory May Day speech in Hyde Park, in which he said that the army should not fire on the workers and that the Union Jack had for generations protected nothing but fools and rogues. The railway companies were reporting increased numbers of volunteers.[7] The bus services in London were beginning to improve with regular

A soldier guarding a bus while on its round during the General Strike

By permission of the National Museum of Labour History

services operating on the no. 1 and no. 2 routes, with volunteer drivers, wire meshing around the driver's seat, and, occasionally, with a policeman or soldier as a guard.

It was also clear that the government wished to break the blockade that the unions exerted over the London docks. There was no doubt that the authorities wished to open Hay's Wharf, for they ferried in blackleg labour, mainly in the form of undergraduates from Oxford and Cambridge, and the appearance of armoured cars, manned by troops, in London heightened speculation about the desire to move food from the docks to Hyde Park.

Indeed, dockland was practically at a standstill and was referred to as the 'Great Silent City of Dockland' in an article which maintained that 'The whole East End of London is a great silent city, even quieter and more peaceful than on Sunday. Not a workshop, factory, or commercial

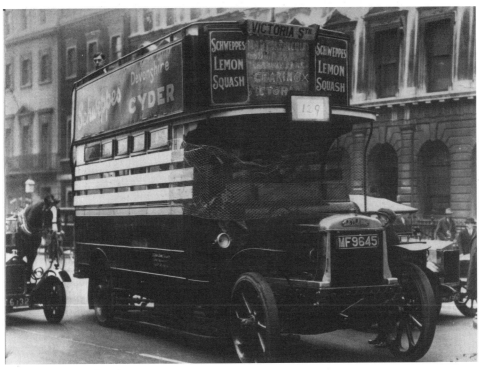

A wired-up bus

By permission of the TUC

concern of any kind is doing business.'[8] One strike bulletin went so far as to suggest that 'The position on the industrial front is, at the moment of writing, most reassuring. Dockland, England's Commercial gateway is stagnant – even the Rats are starving.'[9]

This was not quite the case in other dock areas, for hundreds of students began to flood into the docks as volunteers. Indeed, it was on 6 May that Henry Duckworth took a 'sampling of the fittest and ablest in Cambridge' to Dover.[10] The class nature of the strike became immediately obvious: 'Birkin, our chauffeur, plus a guard for the return journey, was ordered to be round at the Great Gate with his 100 m.p.h. Bentley at five o'clock. Birkin had removed his windscreen in case he should have a brickbat thrown at him . . . since he was not actually a member of the so-called "Dover Fifty" .'[11]

Despite the solidarity of the strikers the TUC and the Labour Party

Pickets outside the London docks

By permission of the National Museum of Labour History

Outside the India Dock gate

By permission of the National Museum of Labour History

began to take urgent steps to encourage new negotiations. Ramsay MacDonald met A.J. Cook and Herbert Smith in the House of Commons to see whether there was a way out of the dispute which the miners could accept. Cook was later caught by the journalists, after a Miners' Executive meeting and outside the House of Commons, and suggested that he thought the strike would last a fortnight. Sir Herbert Samuel, who had just arrived in Dover and been driven to London in less than an hour by Major Harry Seagrave, the champion race driver, contacted Jimmy Thomas to meet the TUC Negotiating Committee on 7 May.

The TUC also replied to Baldwin's speech in a conciliatory tone, while attempting to establish that it had not been responsible for the

Strikers stopping a van with petrol entering the London docks
By permission of the National Museum of Labour History

breakdown of negotiations that led to the General Strike. It reiterated its position and willingness to negotiate.

> The General Council is ready, at any moment, to resume negotiations for an honourable settlement. It enforces no conditions for resuming preliminary discussion with the Government on any aspect of the case.
>
> It is obvious, however, that at this stage, with no knowledge of the subsequent line of policy that the Government intends to pursue, the General Council cannot comply with the Prime Minister's request for an unconditional withdrawal of the strike notices.[12]

The arrival of the *Mauretania* at Southampton. Volunteers loading luggage

By permission of the Illustrated London News *Picture Library*

This was a line which, despite its suggestion of a conciliatory but firm stand, was out of tune with what rank and file organisations throughout the country were demanding. Their message was one of a 'Government . . . at its wit's end to devise ways of breaking our "United Front"'and one of 'WORKERS STAND BY YOUR CLASS' as German, French, Dutch and Belgian workers gave the British workers their support.[13]

Brave words, of course, were not sufficient to win the strike and the TUC had begun a course of action that would ultimately lead to settlement. All that was clear by the end of 6 May was the government's determination to end the blockade of the docks and the TUC's commitment to an early settlement. Both developments began to move apace from 6 May onwards.

Friday 7 May

The dominating features of the fourth full day of the strike were the continuing assertiveness of the government and the tentative peace moves being made by the TUC. There was no doubt by now that it was the government that was taking the offensive.

Government action took four main forms. The first of these was to issue a statement to the effect that any worker continuing to do his work would be protected from any victimisation once the dispute was ended, a promise which the government sought to implement. Addressed 'To all workers in all Trades' it stated that:

> When the present General Strike is ended his Majesty's Government will take effectual measures to prevent the victimisation by Trade Unions of any man who remains at work or who may return to work; and no settlement will be agreed to by His Majesty's Government which does not provide for this for a lasting period and for its enforcement, if necessary, by penalties.
>
> No man who does his duty loyally to the country in the present crisis will be left unprotected by the State from subsequent reprisals.[1]

This statement was subsequently reproduced on several occasions in the *British Gazette* (whose circulation had risen to 655,000) and also reproduced in the forty or so newspapers that were still publishing despite the strike action of the printers.

How much influence this statement exerted on the public mind is difficult to assess. Nevertheless, it must have exerted some on the success of the second government strategy in improving the vital services. In London there was a reasonably successful attempt to get the underground services back in operation. The London General Omnibus Company, which had eighty buses working on 6 May, managed to increase its service even though forty-seven of the buses had been damaged by the strikers. There were also 2,778 trains reported as running, including the first main line train from Edinburgh to London, which left at 10 a.m., though there was no certainty that it would arrive until the next day. The local newspapers that were able to publish continued to request that volunteers should come forward. In West Bromwich it was stated that

> An appeal has been made to all well disposed people to volunteer help in the maintenance of the public services and throughout the country the response has been magnificent. The men and women of West Bromwich will not be behind those of other districts in their readiness to help their country in this great crisis. The local recruiting office is in the Committee Room B at the Town Hall, West Bromwich, and a large number of men and women of all classes have already registered, not of course as strike breakers, but in the interests of the community generally. Hours of Registration 9 a.m. to 2 p.m.[2]

Not surprisingly, then, the cabinet was happy that 'there were ample of supplies of food, transport, and petrol, and that the Supply and Transport Organisation was working smoothly'. However, it remained concerned about the level of picketing.

> The most serious need of the moment, however, was more protection, in view of the intimidation already carried out and threatened. The Trades Union Council had not prohibited the movement of flour and the National Union of Railwaymen had ordered permits for this movement of food stuffs to be controlled. This means stronger measures would be taken in the direction of picketing and docks and other food supplies.[3]

Indeed, the government did act. Joynson-Hicks' appeal for 30,000 more special constables for London had yielded 20,000 men in the previous two days. In the evening a whole fleet of army trucks passed along the Embankment with armoured car escorts, apparently heading for the London docks, although they do not seem to have got there.

The third strategy was for the government to consider the need for new legislation to deal with the strike and the rising level of riots and disturbances. On 7 May the cabinet instructed its lawyers, Birkenhead,

Cave and Hogg, to consider 'what legislation, if any, to strengthen the powers of the Government is necessary and possible, either at the present juncture or in the near future'. This committee of lawyers was clearly formed in response to Simon's parliamentary speech of the previous evening. It suggested the immediate introduction of a three-clause bill 'declaring' as illegal any sympathetic strike action designed to 'coerce the Government or community', the control of union funds and the prevention of the expulsion of trade union members who refused to participate in the strike.[4] In the meantime it was felt that Simon's speech so strongly supported the government position that it would be published on 8 May.

Fourthly, the government was also in the business of denying access to publicity for alternative viewpoints. The Archbishop of Canterbury had issued a statement that: 'Representatives of the Christian Churches are convinced that a real settlement will only be achieved in a spirit of fellowship and co-operation for the common good and not as a result of war. Realising that the longer the present trouble persists the greater will be the suffering and loss, they earnestly request that all parties concerned in the dispute will agree to resume negotiations.'[5]

The proposal was, effectively, for a return to the *status quo* of the previous week, including the cancellation of the General Strike, a short period of government subsidy and the withdrawal by the mine owners of the new reduced wage scales. The initiative was ignored in Churchill's *British Gazette* and John Reith, managing director of the BBC, decided not to broadcast it under the implied threat of Winston Churchill and J.C.C. Davidson that the government would take over the BBC if it were broadcast.

These various strategies strengthened the government but did little to reduce the level of minor violence that was occurring throughout the country. Cardiff strikers attempted to interfere with volunteers driving a tram, and there was violence in Hull as strikers attempted to stop the movement of trams from the Hull docks and as 1,000 men and women attempted to interfere with the recruitment of volunteers at city hall. There was violence in Glasgow and eighty-nine people were arrested.[6] There were also minor scuffles at Dover where the Cambridge undergraduates, the 'Dover Fifty', were installed for the loading and unloading of ships by the Southern Railway Company.

In this climate of unrest and government aggression the TUC

attempted to calm matters and prepare the way for a settlement. Its Negotiating Committee, led by Jimmy Thomas, began to meet Sir Herbert Samuel behind closed doors at the house of Sir Abe Bailey in Bryanston Square. In the meantime, it was denied that the TUC and the Labour Party were attempting to reopen negotiations on the basis that the General Council had had 'no direct or indirect communications with the Government'.[7] Nevertheless, it was declared that: 'The position of the General Council may be stated in simple and unequivocal terms. They are ready at any moment to enter into preliminary discussions regarding the withdrawal of the lockout notices and the ending of the General Stoppage and the resumption of negotiations for an honourable settlement of the Mining Dispute. These preliminary discussions must be free from any condition.' In response to rumblings about the unconstitutional nature of the General Strike it added that: 'The General Council does not challenge the Constitution. It is not seeking to substitute unconstitutional government. Nor is it desirous of undermining our Parliamentary institutions. The sole aim of the Council is to secure for all the miners a decent standard of life. The Council is engaged in an Industrial dispute. *There is no Constitutional crisis.*'

The TUC was also adamant that the strike was generally peaceful and widely supported. An interesting insight into this sense of unity occurred in Gloucester where the NUR Women's Guild, ASLEF Women's Society and the Transport Women's Guild held a mass meeting in a marquee on the Labour Club lawns to support the strike effort. It was presided over by Mr Potlock, and attended by Mrs Prosser JP and Mr Charles Fox. After hearing a stirring account of the lives of miners the chairman, seconded by Mrs Smart, carried unanimously the motion 'That we, the wives of Trade Unionists, pledge our loyal support to the men engaged in the present conflict and urge them to continue steadfast in their endeavour to obtain justice for the miners and their wives.'[8] The meeting also raised £1 6s 11d for the Strikers' Relief Fund.

Nevertheless, the TUC found one major problem connected with its administration, and that was the issue of permits. The TUC had argued that their issue should be co-ordinated through the NUR headquarters at Euston Road but on 6 May, because of the inconsistency of treatment, it was decided that they should be reviewed by local transport committees. This was difficult since most councils of action had assumed that they had the right to issue them and to control the movement of goods or to agree to strikers remaining at work. Mindful of this confusion the National Transport Committee, consisting of all the transport unions, circulated telegrams to the local transport committees on 7 May. The following was sent to Liverpool.

7.15 P.M. LONDON CTO
EDWARDS ENGINEERS HALL MOUNT PLEASANT LV WE INSTRUCT ALL LOCAL TRANSPORT COMMITTEES REVIEW ALL PERMITS WHICH HAVE BEEN ISSUED NO TRADES COUNCIL LABOUR PARTY COUNCIL OF ACTION STRIKE COMMITTEE OR TRADE UNION BRANCH HAS AUTHORITY TO DEAL WITH THE PERMITS PLEASE CONVEY TO ALL CONCERNED + NATIONAL TRANSPORT COMMITTEE UNITY HOUSE LONDON[9]

The telegram clarified the issue but did little to solve the problem.

The General Council was also faced with the difficulty of continuing to operate the *British Worker*. Although the government allowed it to continue production Churchill requisitioned the bulk of its newsprint. Therefore, it had to reduce its length from eight pages to four from now onwards and was only able to continue production as a result of acquiring newsprint from the *Racing and Football Outlook*, the *New Leader* and Lansbury's *Labour Weekly*.[10]

While the strike was still holding up well there were signs that the government was increasing its control and contemplating legislation to ban general strikes. Yet by this stage the General Council was viewing a possible settlement with some haste and eagerness.

SATURDAY 8 MAY

The first really dramatic moment in the General Strike was seen on 8 May when the government moved to break the picketing that had placed a stranglehold on the London docks. It was, indeed, a day which belonged to the government, with the prime minister broadcasting to the nation, Lord Oxford and Asquith supporting the government, and with the publication of Sir John Simon's speech delivered in the House of Commons on 6 May.

The pickets had stopped the London docks functioning properly since the beginning of the strike. Until Saturday 8 May, it looked as though food supplies could be paralysed, and London was down to only forty-eight hours' supply of flour and bread. At this juncture the government, which had been gathering armoured cars and troops in London for the

A food convoy proceeding down East India Dock Road, London, led by armoured cars
By permission of the National Museum of Labour History

previous few days, sprang into action. At 4 a.m., 20 armoured cars left Hyde Park to escort 105 lorries through the West End and the City of London to the docks. Volunteers had been ferried to the docks by lighter to avoid the pickets who had blocked the roads. It took three hours to load the lorries while Grenadier Guardsmen took charge of the Docks area. At 11.20 a.m. the lorries came back fully laden. The pickets and the strikers of the East End watched in silence as the convoy passed and there was little disturbance as the lorries made their way back to Hyde Park. Once in the park the armoured cars made themselves ready for another convoy while the food was unloaded for distribution. The whole episode was a well-organised operation which demonstrated the government's overall control of the strike situation. The message was clear; it was the government that was in control. It would brook no serious opposition.

Prime Minister Baldwin followed up this success with a speech on the BBC that evening in which he presented himself as ' a man of peace'. He said, 'I do not believe that any honest person can doubt that my whole desire is to maintain the standard of living of every worker, and that I am ready to press the employers to make any sacrifice to this end, consistent with keeping industry itself in working order.' There was no door closed to negotiations, he insisted: 'I am a man of peace. I am longing and working and praying for peace, but I will not surrender the safety and security of the British Constitution. You placed me in power eighteen months ago by the largest majority accorded to any party for many, many years. Have I done anything to forfeit that confidence? Cannot you trust me to ensure a square deal to secure even justice between man and man?'[1]

Baldwin had already received support earlier in the day from a former Liberal prime minister, H.H. Asquith who, as Lord Oxford and Asquith, had spoken in the House of Lords and written in support of the government and against the foolishness of the General Strike.[2] Baldwin had also decided to form a Constabulary Force for London, a Civil Constabulary Reserve, which could be likened to the territorial army. Interestingly, General Sir George Milne had jumped the gun and personally arrested a newspaper seller he heard in Lower Berkeley Square, London, shouting 'Great Public Revolution: The Army has refused to fight.' The newspaper man was remanded in custody.

The cabinet was still also considering the need for a bill to ban the General Strike to be introduced on Tuesday 11 May, although it could be

Troops in convoy moving through the City of London

By permission of the National Museum of Labour History

made effective by 10 May. It was also contemplating the need to extend its powers under the Emergency Powers Act through the Privy Council, on 9 May, to control the trade union funds.

All was not well with the government-organised attempts to break the strike though, for volunteer drivers were beginning to cause concern. There were many minor accidents beginning to occur on the railways. One such accident, which occurred on the Huddersfield and Manchester line, was not untypical: 'Six trains passed through Huddersfield on Saturday. The 8.30 a.m. train to Manchester collided with the level crossing gates at Clayton Bridge. Only slight damage was done. The train was able to proceed.'[3]

Yet the TUC was now very much more on the defensive than it had been at any point hitherto in the dispute. Stung by Sir John Simon's criticism of the previous Thursday, and the government's publication of the speech on the previous day, it expressed its views through the *British Worker*. It denied that the General Strike was an 'attack on the community'. Indeed, its statement ran as follows:

Misleading the Nation
Our Reply to Sir John Simon's Innuendos and Charges

In his speech in the House of Commons on Thursday Sir John Simon made much play with the statement that in ceasing to work on Monday night certain workers had broken their contracts with their employers. He went on to argue that this proved that a general stoppage differed essentially from a stoppage in a single industry. He concluded by saying that 'the attack on the community' had 'deprived the miners of a great deal of sympathy they thoroughly deserved'. The same speech was broadcast this morning.

There is, as far as the Trade Union Movement is concerned, no 'attack on the community'. There is no 'attempt to set up a rival Government'. There is no 'challenge to the Constitution'. The workers have exercised their legal and long-established right of withholding their labour, in order to protect the miners against a degradation of their standard of life, which is a menace to the whole world of labour.[4]

In the meantime, the TUC was deeply embroiled in the discussions with Sir Herbert Samuel. At this juncture, Samuel informed the TUC Negotiating Committee that 'ministers were not prepared to negotiate either privately or openly'.[5] Later in the day the cabinet was informed that Sir Arthur Steel-Maitland, minister of labour, had, on 7 May, sent a letter to Samuel explaining the position of the government. It said that:

We have repeatedly stated that we cannot negotiate until the General Strike has been withdrawn. . . .

In these circumstances, I am sure that the Government will take the view that while they are forced most carefully and most sympathetically to consider the terms of any arrangement which a public man of your responsibility and experience may prepare, it is important to make it plain that any decision which you think proper to initiate is not clothed in even the vestige of official character.[6]

This was the position which the government maintained to the end of the dispute and of which the TUC Negotiating Committee was aware, although it agreed to keep the government rebuff from the miners and their colleagues on the General Council and continued to contemplate an arrangement whereby, if a settlement could be worked out in detail, wage reductions would be conceded if the government provided a temporary subsidy.

Samuel continued his talks with the TUC Negotiating Committee and the first version of the 'Samuel Memorandum' was circulated to the General Council on the evening of 8 May, and shown to the miners the following day. It was broadly based on the Samuel Report, with demands for the reorganisation of the coal industry and wage reductions for one year, but included the added device of an impartial National Wages Board to maintain a watch over the reorganisation of the industry and the local wage arrangements that might be agreed.[7]

The General Strike continued to produce its regular mixture of violence, disturbance, peaceful activity and moments of truce. The Tottenham Trades Council Emergency Committee called for 'NO COMPROMISE WITH THE WEAKLINGS – ALL POWER TO THE WORKERS' and was concerned that the strikers should not forget the lesson of 1921 when there was a lack of unity.[8] There was continued violence in many areas, such as Edinburgh. There was trouble at Preston with stone throwing at the buses by a crowd of 4,000 or so who had been warned by the chief constable to disperse. In the end the police arrested six people. There was also major conflict in Newcastle between the police and a crowd of 10,000 people at which twenty-four arrests were made. Also, at Winlaton Mills, nearby, a police inspector, four sergeants and sixteen constables arrested two men who attempted to interfere with food distribution. They were Henry Bolton and William Lawther. Lawther argued that food could not be distributed without the permits issued by the council of action and Bolton threatened to get 200 men from his village to stop them. Both were arrested and sent to Durham Gaol. Lawther had a copy of the *Northern Light* which contained the words, 'We must do all in our power to keep the peace, but we must unceasingly demand the resignation of the Government. Bevin, Smith, and Cook ought to take the reins of Government in the interest of the whole people.'[9] Bolton was a JP on Durham County Council and Lawther was a prominent member of the Labour Party National Executive at that time.

It was also on this day that one of the most celebrated events of the strike took place. At Plymouth the starting of a tram service had led to disturbances and a volunteer driver had been dragged from the platform of his tram and roughly handled. Matters grew worse in the afternoon, but many strikers were drawn off to witness a football match between the strikers and the police. The chief constable's wife kicked off, even though some people felt that football was inappropriate to the gravity of the country's situation, and the strikers beat the police 2–1.

A resolute government and a weakening TUC characterised 8 May. Indeed, the government was allowing the TUC to talk and work itself into a position of capitulation. Partly in tune with its desire to avoid any association with violence, and partly to dissociate itself from revolutionary communism, the TUC General Council returned the £26,000 sent to it by the General Council of the Unions of the USSR. Yet the TUC was reluctant to act without some form of guarantee that a settlement would open up serious negotiations in the coal mining industry.

The football teams at Plymouth

By permission of the Illustrated London News *Picture Library*

SUNDAY 9 MAY

This was the first, and indeed only, Sunday of the General Strike and the level of picketing and violence appears to have been rather less than usual. Nevertheless, the government pushed home its breakthrough of the picketing on dockland and there was some significant propagandising going on, by both sides. It also became even clearer that the negotiations between Samuel and the TUC were unlikely to win the support of the miners for a settlement.

The government particularly emphasised the breakthrough it had made in docklands. It was reported that: 'Complete confidence and order are maintained throughout London dock area. Convoys are moving freely in and out of the docks. The work of loading and unloading vessels by volunteer labour is proceeding and increasing continually.' Indeed, 'No difficulty was experienced in the revictualling of London, and it is intended to keep the Port of London regularly opened. In general the situation at all ports is distinctly better than last week.'[1] This is, perhaps, not surprising given that it was reported that a convoy of 158 trucks had got through from the docks to Hyde Park on 9 May. The government also drew comfort from the fact that the situation in Scotland had improved, despite some rioting in Glasgow and Edinburgh. The London Underground was also working more effectively than before. Cardinal Bourne, the Roman Catholic Archbishop of Westminster, also laid down the moral principles for Catholics during this unprecedented situation, which reflected his view that the General Strike was a sin against God.

Counterbalancing the military display associated with the convoys, the TUC stated that it was as patriotic as anybody and was not out to attack the Constitution. In addition, thousands of trade unionists decided to wear their military service medals and ribbons. Several strike bulletins reminded their rank and file supporters to 'Remember the Sabbath Day to keep it Holy'.[2] Also, at a press conference, the TUC replied to Mr Baldwin's broadcast of 8 May. The TUC spokesman said that no door is

Huts being erected as accommodation for staff working in Hyde Park, London
By permission of the Illustrated London News *Picture Library*

closed: 'If the door is open, it is for the Prime Minister to make it clear that the lockout notices should be withdrawn as well as the General Strike cancelled.' The *British Worker* added that 'The General Council has never closed any door that might be kept open for negotiations. It has done nothing to imperil the food supplies; on the contrary, its members were instructed to co-operate with the Government in maintaining them. No notice has been taken of the offer.'[3] The comment was in fact fair and accurate, although the government had already made it clear to Sir Herbert Samuel that it was not prepared to negotiate while the strike continued.

Samuel in fact replied to Steel-Maitland's earlier letter, received on 8 May, and wrote: 'Let me take the opportunity to put on record the assurance I gave you in conversation that, in discussions which I have had on the present situation I have made it perfectly clear that I have been acting entirely on my own initiative and without any kind of

Workers loading milk supplies into lorries in Hyde Park, London
By permission of the National Museum of Labour History

authorisation from the Government. I am quite satisfied that there has been no possibility of misunderstanding on that point. In any further communication that may take place I still, of course, maintain the same attitude.'[4]

The door at Sir Abe Bailey's house in Bryanston Square was in fact constantly opening and closing as the discussions developed that day. Nevertheless, on 9 May the prospect that the miners might accept some type of wage cuts implied in the Samuel discussions was looking increasingly remote. On the late Saturday evening or early Sunday morning the miners' leaders were presented with a written draft of the Samuel proposals. Herbert Smith dismissed them as 'a new suit of clothes for the same body', but called up his executive to meet the General Council that night. Walter Citrine recorded his own mood and that of the TUC leaders.

It was evident to me that the General Council were coming to the conclusion that it was simply hopeless to continue the strike if the intention was that in no circumstances and in no conditions would the miners accept any reductions. We cannot see any possibility of winning on this negative issue, yet we are still all apprehensive of what will follow after the miners have been told that they cannot, in the view of the General Council, hope to secure an undertaking that there will be reduction. . . . It will be a repetition of Black Friday, with the difference that we will have had the General Strike, and we will have realised either our strength or our impotence.[5]

He further suggested that there was little likelihood of getting terms that the miners could agree to, although he clung to the hope that the General Strike might force a subsidy out of the government to ease the way for the miners to settle.

The pessimistic and conciliatory mood of the TUC leaders had already been telegraphed by two speeches which Jimmy Thomas made during the day. Speaking at Camden Town, he rejected the idea that the General Council was threatening the Constitution, arguing that 'the constitutional issue is as foolish as it is untrue. It is dangerous. It is foolish because no one knows better than the Government that we have not, that we will not, no matter how long the battle, attempt to supersede this Government. . . .'[6] In his more famous, and much misrepresented, speech at King's Hall, Hammersmith, in the afternoon he said that he had 'never been in favour of the General Strike'.[7] His main point, however, was that no one ever wanted a General Strike but that it had become inevitable. In addition, he stated that: 'It is the duty of both sides to keep the door open. . . . The task is a difficult one. The responsibility is a heavy one. But there will be a graver responsibility on whichever side fails to recognise the moment when an honourable settlement can be arrived at. The moment must be accepted and everyone must work to that end.' Thomas' speech was in fact consistent with his position throughout the strike. At the outset he had been looking for industrial peace and a negotiated settlement.

The Sunday night meeting between the General Council and the miners' executive was unproductive. The General Council insisted that no settlement was possible without wage reductions while the miners' leaders simply rejected wage cuts. As Cook wrote later: 'On Sunday, May 9th it was quite evident that these discussions and pow wows had reached a stage where the Negotiating Committee and the leaders of the Labour Party felt that something tangible had been secured to justify a move towards calling off the General Strike.'[8] The miners remained unconvinced of that likelihood. They were, nevertheless, dragged into a meeting with Samuel, who recited the proposals. Cook rejected them immediately, much to the surprise of Samuel who had been led to believe that the miners were prepared to accept wage cuts if there were guarantees about the reorganisation of the coal industry.

In the meantime Thomas's busy day of meetings with Samuel and the miners, and his speeches, was capped by a number of meetings with Lord Wimborne and Lord Reading where he conveyed to them the possibility of the TUC calling off the General Strike if guarantees could be given about the reorganisation of the coal industry. The message was conveyed back to Baldwin who swept the suggestions aside, since he felt that he had given enough guarantees. Nevertheless, Baldwin must have become very aware that the TUC was desperate to call off the strike.

Apart from these major developments the strike lumbered on, with the usual claims to unity, organised mass meetings as occurred in the Peckham Winter Gardens and at Bradford, where 10,000 people turned up, and the routine disturbances.[9] The rioting continued in Glasgow and the total number of arrests rose to about 200 between Thursday and Saturday.

The government was gradually extending its control and influence over the vital food supplies of the nation and was resolutely determined not to negotiate until the strike was called off. Equally, it is clear that Thomas and many of the other leading members of the General Council were perceptibly moving towards a settlement based on a version of the Samuel Report. What was delaying their progress was the fact that the miners' leaders were not prepared to accept any terms that meant reduced pay and longer hours. Until the General Council decided what it was going to do about the miners there was not likely to be a settlement. The choice was a stark one: either the General Council had to continue to support the miners, in which case the General Strike would continue, or it had to abandon them in the hope that negotiations would be reopened as the miners faced reality.

MONDAY 10 MAY

Three events dominated 10 May and stood above the rest of the normal pattern of industrial disturbance. First of all, the miners rejected the Samuel Memorandum on both 9 and 10 May, but offered what proved an unacceptable alternative arrangement. Secondly, there was the dramatic derailing of the 'Flying Scotsman' near Newcastle. Thirdly, there was the decision of the cabinet not to proceed with a bill to make general strikes illegal; it evidently felt that the strike was drawing to a close and was influenced partly by the TUC's continuing desperate attempts to get a settlement.

On 9 and 10 May the TUC Negotiating Committee raised the possibility of a new agreement in which wage reductions would be implemented only after the reorganisation of the coal industry had occurred. Yet the miners' leaders would not consider anything which involved a wage cut. As Walter Citrine wrote of this meeting, on the evening of Monday 10 May: 'Miner after miner got up and, speaking with an intensity of feeling, affirmed that the miners could not go back to work on a reduction in wages.' Arthur Pugh, putting the TUC view, suggested that the miners were 'living in a fool's paradise' and that they would be defeated by 'a process of attrition'.[1] Ultimately, after an adjournment, the miners accepted the Samuel agreement as long as the TUC included a statement to the effect that they saw no reason for wage reductions since reorganisation would make them unnecessary.[2] The TUC was unwilling to take any such action since Samuel would have found that difficult to accept, as would the employers and the government. In effect, it would still have preserved the objection of the miners to wage reductions.

Such problems were hidden from a watching public who were unaware that secret peace talks were occurring. Far more obvious was the derailing of the 'Flying Scotsman', the London express from Edinburgh, which was wrecked in the afternoon between Annitsford and

Cramlington, a few miles north of Newcastle, with 500 to 600 passengers on board.[3] Only one passenger was hurt. The train, with one engine and fifteen coaches, left Edinburgh at 10 a.m. Nothing untoward occurred until it was about three-quarters of a mile north of Dam Dyke level crossing when the train had slowed down to six miles per hour. The volunteer driver, 'Bob' Sheldon, and his fireman Robert Aitken, of Edinburgh University, saw that a rail had been removed but were unable to brake quickly enough to prevent an accident. The engine left the rails and plunged into a disused signal cabin at the side. The guard's van, too, was thrown on its side while the coach immediately behind turned to right angles with the rails. However, the remaining section of the train remained on the rails and so a major catastrophe was avoided. Although some coaches caught fire the situation was soon brought under control.

The police were convinced that the accident had been deliberate, for part of the railway with two iron bars and a sledge hammer were discovered near the track. There was also a crowd of men and women,

Train drivers putting out the fires after the derailment of the 'Flying Scotsman', the Edinburgh to London express, 10 May 1926

By permission of the National Museum of Labour History

presumably from nearby Cramlington, waving and jeering at the passengers until they were taken by taxis, buses and private cars to Newcastle.

Yet this day also brought less spectacular but more serious accidents. Three people were killed in a train accident on the 1.06 p.m. from Berwick to Edinburgh, when a passenger train ran into a goods train. A goods train from Cambridge ran into a passenger train at Bishop's Stortford, two coaches were derailed and one man was killed.[4] Volunteer train drivers clearly had their limitations.

Despite such dramatic railway accidents it is clear that the railways were beginning to offer an expanding minimum service, even if it was not always well used and maintained by management and volunteers. Indeed, the railway companies were becoming more aggressive and were proposing to issue a notice to their staff to the effect that 'Members of staff who have absented themselves from duty, without giving the notice prescribed by the terms of their service, are warned that unless they offer to resume work by (a date to be inserted) steps will be taken to fill their vacant places.'[5] Despite this it was reported that 4,253 trains were running throughout the country and that the 'Big Four' railway companies were running about 3,700 of these.[6] The passenger numbers were poor but the freight services ensured that food supplies were being properly distributed. Indeed, the Great Western Railway claimed to have delivered twice the quantity of milk it normally delivered to London, to such an extent that the authorities were becoming worried that there was a milk surplus in London.

The government and the authorities, indeed, seemed to be in control of the dispute. It was reported that volunteers were manning the meat markets at Smithfield and that under police protection they were moving up to three times the normal number of carcasses. Convoys of food were still moving from London docks to Hyde Park and then out to other areas in London. Indeed, there was almost a sense of resignation in the *British Worker* when the General Council appealed for the workers to stand firm and when a description of the armoured convoys was given, presumably drawn from a report of events on 9 May, although the timing is not given. The description of the latter situation was presented in an almost laconic fashion.

At London Termini and in Dockland
To-and-fro Engines: Armed Convoys in Silent Thames-side

. . . I pushed on through Hackney, Dalston, into Poplar and Canning Town. All along the route I passed thousands of strikers with hands in their pockets, many wearing badges; but no work was in progress anywhere.

In the dock areas were policemen in twos and threes. They were more numerous than in the other districts I had come through.

At the Iron Bridge, at Canning Town, I met a half company of soldiers, tin-hatted, and with rifles and packs, marching into the docks.

Food convoy with troop escort

By permission of the National Museum of Labour History

Troops moving through Poplar with armoured cars and lorries

By permission of the National Museum of Labour History

I circled round past several of the big dock gates. All were closed and guarded by policemen and pickets....

Inside the docks not a man was visible. Cranes, derricks and gantries stood pointing heavenward, still and silent. No rattle of winch or hauling-gear broke the silence.

I returned back through the Iron Bridge. A big crowd had gathered, mounted police lined the road, foot police were in plenty, with half-a-dozen platoons of soldiers on either side at 200 yard intervals.

The Convoy Passes

'What's happening?' I asked one of the spectators.

'The convoy is coming', was the reply, and just then up came an armoured car, lorries of meat, lorries of soldiers, more soldiers; an armoured car brought up the rear.

I learnt from one of the dockers' pickets that about 150 tons of meat had been taken overnight from one of the ships, and was now being moved by this unnecessary display of force.

The men, whose normal work is to handle thousands of tons of such cargo each day, line the streets with arms folded, smiling and chatting, some waving a greeting to the soldiers.[7]

The overwhelming mood seemed to be one of resignation and a desire for settlement. Indeed, the British Worker expressed this sentiment in an article which referred to a more recent sermon by the Archbishop of Canterbury given at St Martin-in-the-Fields. The TUC was equally determined to suggest that it was prepared to reopen negotiations with the government, which the government had abandoned, and emphasised that there had been no direct negotiations with the government since the beginning of the dispute.[8]

It was at this juncture that the *British Worker* began producing a Manchester edition, edited by Fenner Brockway. Another edition was produced in Cardiff and South Wales. However, it was the Manchester edition which became most popular, eventually reaching a circulation of about 50,000.

A mass meeting at Reading during the General Strike

By permission of the TUC

The rank and file mood still remained enthusiastic. The AEU Strike Committee was meeting regularly in Preston and in Aberdeen: 'The railwaymen were solid; no trains running. . . . The docks are out solidly.'[9] The local enthusiasm for the strike was still there. Yet it was the national, rather than the local, organisations that were going to make the vital decisions.

The government clearly considered the possibility of a bill to make general strikes illegal, an action sponsored by the hawks in the cabinet. However, perhaps given the way in which the TUC leaders were angling for a settlement, it was decided that 'the moment for its introduction was not quite opportune'.[10]

It is clear that the government now felt that the settlement of the dispute was near and that the TUC General Council would act to deliver it as soon as possible. There remained, however, the tricky problem of dealing with the mining situation as quickly as possible.

Waiting to buy coal at the GER coal depot in the East End of London
By permission of the Illustrated London News *Picture Library*

Tuesday 11 May

Despite the fact that thousands of second line workers were to be called out to strengthen the dispute on 12 May all the evidence is that the TUC was trying to bring the industrial conflict to a speedy conclusion. As a result there was much coming and going at Eccleston Square throughout the day. This change of mood was noted at 12 noon by a government spokesman who said that 'Without being unduly optimistic, the tide has turned.' At 7 p.m. the government noted that, 'The situation throughout the country shows a further improvement and the government prides itself that order and quiet reign throughout the whole island.'[1] Despite this classic exaggeration and all the countercurrents throughout of the day it was industrial peace that was expected.

The miners did not help matters. The TUC Negotiating Committee met Samuel on the morning of 11 May to suggest that the miners were unmovable, and met him again in the afternoon to form what became the final version of the Samuel Memorandum. Then Samuel went away to secure the signatures of his former colleagues on the Coal Commission, which he failed to achieve because of their fundamental opposition to the renewal of the subsidy.

Samuel was also clearly in touch with the government, for Steel-Maitland, the minister of labour, made clear, once again, that:

> Until the necessary orders have been given to withdraw the Strike or unless the Strike has come to an end we cannot as a condition or inducement take part in negotiations in relation to the mining issue . . . [the government] hold that the General Strike is unconstitutional and illegal. They are bound to take steps to make its repetition impossible. . . . In these circumstances I am sure that the government will take a view that while they are bound most carefully and most sympathetically to consider the terms of an arrangement which public men of your responsibility and

experience may propose, it is imperative to make it plain that any discussion which you think proper to initiate is not clothed in even a vestige of official character.[2]

In the meantime, the General Council met the miners on the evening of the 11 May, indicating that the memorandum was a 'fair basis for negotiating a settlement'. Again, Cook reveals the extent to which the miners felt suspicious of the whole process of negotiation:

> We were told these proposals were unalterable, could not be amended, that we had to accept them *en bloc* as this was the unanimous decision of the TUC.
>
> Mr Pugh was continually pressed and questioned by Mr Herbert Smith, myself, and my colleagues about what the guarantees mentioned were, and who had given them. We got no answers. But J.H. Thomas said to me personally, when I asked him whether the Government would accept the Samuel proposals, and who were his guarantors: 'You may not trust my word, but will you accept the word of a British Gentleman who has been Governor of Palestine?'[3]

After that meeting, with a two-hour recess, the miners rejected the Samuel Memorandum, for they could not agree to wage reductions, and objected to the General Council decision to end the dispute. Thereafter, the General Council asked Citrine to organise an interview with the prime minister for noon on 12 May. According to Citrine a telephone call from Patrick Gower, one of the prime minister's secretaries, indicated that Baldwin 'wants to know whether you have any news for him. He has been sitting up for you. Do you want to see him this evening?' After consulting the General Council, Citrine replied that: '"The General Council instruct me to say that they will be ready to see the Prime Minister tomorrow at twelve o'clock noon, positively." "All right, Mr Citrine, we may take that as fixed." Our fate was decided in those few seconds. Our decision to see the Prime Minister meant plainly to them the calling off of the General Strike.'[4] The end of the strike was arranged for 12 o'clock on the Wednesday, 12 May 1926.

This development made the attempts of Sir John Simon, and some sections of the Liberal Party, to speed up the end of the dispute somewhat irrelevant. In an attempt to restore balance to the Liberal Party's approach, following Simon's outburst against the strike on 6 May, Simon and some Liberal MPs put down a Commons motion calling for a simultaneous withdrawal of both the strike and the lockout, the unrestricted acceptance of the Samuel Report by the government, miners and coal owners, and the renewal of a subsidy for a brief period.[5]

These rapid moves towards a settlement of the dispute were barely reflected in the public presentation of the TUC's position. It was maintained that there was 'NO SLACKENING' of the effort and that 'The number of strikers has not diminished: it is increasing. There are more workers out to-day than there have been at any moment since the strike began.'[6] Emphasis was also placed on getting the *British Worker* into each centre and each village, for 'There must be no weak link in the chain of dispatch riders from the General Council to each centre, from each centre to each town and village in its area, and from them to every man

Volunteer engine drivers

By permission of the National Museum of Labour History

and woman in the Labour Movement.'[7] The NUR suggested that its members should ignore the reports that thousands of railwaymen were at work and attacked the attempt to induce the men to return to work: 'Personal letters have been addressed to members of staff, and these have, in a number of instances, been followed up by telegrams of mysterious origin, instructing them to report for duty at a certain time.'[8] W. Paling, reporting to the TUC General Council Intelligence Committee on his visits to York and Doncaster, confirmed that 'a fine spirit exists' and that very few trains were running.[9] In addition, 100,000 men were about to down tools in the Scottish engineering and shipbuilding industries, and all was well in both Preston and Reading.[10] In the case of Reading there were 'heartening reports of cheery courage and determination to go forward unflinchingly'. The rhetoric and success and unity could be repeated endlessly, although there were real and serious conflicts from time to time.

A volunteer worker in a railway signal box

By permission of the National Museum of Labour History

Brighton saw its first serious conflict with the Battle of Lewes Road outside the tram depot when 300 police and 50 mounted specials, led by 'Sergeant' Harry Preston, proprietor of the Royal Albion and Royal York Hotel, and Harry Mason, a professional boxer, fought with strikers. This motley collection of ex-cavalry men, ex-black and tans and ex-yeomanry gradually forced the strikers back and there were two injuries and seventeen arrests.[11]

Yet there was mounting evidence of the authorities exerting more control. The *Leviathan* sailed from Southampton to New York with 383 passengers on board, the baggage being shipped by volunteer labour.[12] The Great Western Railway had 276 sets of engineers available for duty on Monday and 316 sets available for Tuesday.[13] As a result of the increased number of volunteers there were 5,079 trains run and 850 buses at work in London.[14] Twenty members of the Birmingham Strike Committee were arrested, including four JPs, because the *Birmingham Strike Bulletin* had issued a false statement to the effect that the government had been defeated in the House of Commons on a motion deleting certain arrests without warrant powers for the emergency

---

GREAT WESTERN RAILWAY.

————

The following special message signed by the Prime Minister to all workers in all trades was broadcast to-day :—

" **Additional Guarantees.**

" Every man who does his duty by the " country and remains at work or returns to work " during the present crisis will be protected by " the State from loss of Trade Union Benefits, " Superannuation Allowances, or Pensions. His " Majesty's Government will take whatever steps " are necessary in Parliament or otherwise for " this purpose."

FELIX J. C. POLE,
General Manager

PADDINGTON STATION,
May 8th, 1926.

A poster issued on 11 May 1926 by the GWR, guaranteeing protection against victimisation to volunteers

By permission of the National Museum of Labour History

regulations. Those arrested included John Strachey and Lesley Plummer, both activists from London. Plummer had been told to publish the statement but Strachey had not checked it for accuracy. *The Times* also reported that it had increased its circulation to 300,000 in the last few days.

During these last-fling skirmishes for control the government was further buoyed up by the Astbury Judgment in the High Court, which supported the National Sailors' and Firemen's Union in its refusal to allow the TUC to order its members to leave work. Astbury argued that the General Strike was 'illegal and contrary to the law', since under the 1906 Trade Union and Trade Disputes Act, 'no trade dispute had been alleged or shown to exist in any case of the unions affiliated, except the miners' case'.[15] Justice Astbury's decision was in fact tacked on to a situation where James Havelock Wilson, president of the Seamen's Union, was attempting to stop the Town Hill branch of his union calling out members in support of the strike on the grounds that a two-thirds majority of members was required for a strike call and because the strike was contrary to the law.

It was now only a matter of hours before the General Strike was going to be called off. The unity of the working classes counted for nothing once the TUC had pinned all its hopes on the Samuel Memorandum.

WEDNESDAY 12 MAY

The events of this day are almost legendary, for they saw the TUC General Council capitulate to the government by calling off the only General Strike in its history. The General Council had convinced itself that the Samuel Memorandum would be a basis for settlement, even though the government had always made it clear that it would not be committed to any arrangement made between Samuel and the TUC. In the end, the TUC was looking for a pretext to settle the dispute and putting the best gloss it could on the decision.

The day began with the TUC and Labour leaders making one more

Herbert Smith (in the cloth cap) and A.J. Cook (second from the right), the miners' leaders during the General Strike

By permission of the TUC

effort to secure the agreement of the miners to the Samuel Memorandum. According to Cook, Ramsay MacDonald asked to talk to the miners' executive but was told that he could not: 'You have already taken your stand in appealing to us to consider reductions and the full acceptance of the Samuel report, which meant reductions. That has been your attitude throughout, and we do not want you to come to our meeting.'[1] Yet Bevin and Purcell headed a six-man delegation to the Russell Square headquarters of the MFGB. Bevin and others urged the miners to agree to the Samuel Memorandum, and argued that their rejection would split the movement. In characteristic style, Herbert Smith argued that the TUC was spending too much time on the doormat of the prime minister. There was no breakthrough being achieved and at 11.45 Bevin left and caught a cab to get to Downing Street to meet the Negotiating Committee of the General Council for their noon meeting with Prime Minister Baldwin.

One of the momentous moments in British trade union history began when the representatives of the General Council went in cars, sporting the official yellow labels of the TUC, from Eccleston Square to 10 Downing Street. To the small crowd that had gathered, they appeared to be glum and despondent. They were met on the doorstep of 10 Downing Street at just after 12 noon (12.10) by Sir Horace Wilson and were only allowed in once the calling off of the General Strike had been more or less confirmed. They then waited a few minutes for Ernest Bevin to return from a last minute meeting with the miners. The subsequent discussions between the TUC and Baldwin are worth recording at length, for they demonstrate how both sides were attempting to restore relations and how Baldwin confined himself to only the broadest and vaguest of commitments.

Mr Pugh: Well, as a result of developments in that direction [industrial peace] and the possibilities that we see in getting back to negotiations and your assurances, speaking for the general community of citizens as a whole, that no stones should be left unturned to get back to negotiations, we are here to-day, sir, to say that this general strike is to be terminated forthwith in order that negotiations may proceed, and we can only hope may proceed in a manner which will bring about a satisfactory settlement. That is the announcement which my General Council is empowered to make.

The Prime Minister: That is, the general strike is to be called off forthwith.

Mr Pugh: . . . Forthwith. That means immediately.

PM: . . . All I would say in answer to that is I thank God for your decision and would now say I do not think it is a moment for a lengthy discussion . . . .

[Mr Thomas asked for help in the return to work]

Mr Bevin: I think you will agree in the difficulties we have had before us, at least we have taken a great risk in calling off the strike. I want to urge it must not be regarded as an act of weakness, but rather one of strength. I am not talking of strength of muscle and brawn, but rather that it took a little courage to take the line we have done. I want to stress Mr Thomas's point and ask if you could tell us whether you are prepared to make a general request as head of the Government that facilitate, etc., really facilitate for reinstatement, and that kind of thing, shall be given forthwith. [This was followed by a long discussion on the problems of economic dislocation which could slow down the rate at which the men were able to return to their work]

I do not know whether I am overstepping the bounds, but I would like you to give me an idea of whether that means that there is to be a resumption of the many operations with us or whether all the negotiations have to be carried on while the miners are still out.

Mr Thomas: That implies that we interpret your speech to mean what I am sure it did mean.

Mr Bevin: It helped us to rise to the occasion.

PM: The point that you have put to me is one I must consider, and I will consider it at once. I would only say in my view the best thing to do is to get on quickly as possible into touch with the employers. I think that the quicker that is done the less friction there will be. You know my record. . . .

In response to the second point there again I cannot say at this moment what will happen because I shall have to see the problems. My object, of course, is to get the mines started at the first possible moment. . . .[2]

One might reflect that Ernest Bevin was rather disappointed by the general tone and progress made in these discussions. He had agreed that the strike should be called off but had also wanted to discuss the resumption of work in detail and the possibility of negotiations based on the Samuel Memorandum, upon which the General Council had hooked itself. The last two requirements had not been discussed in any detail. Bevin was clearly unhappy with developments and is supposed to have said, on leaving 10 Downing Street, that 'There is something wrong here'. He felt that either Samuel had overestimated his influence or that the government had reneged on an agreement. He seems not to have been well informed about the reservations that Samuel had placed upon his discussions and to have discounted the possibility that Jimmy Thomas was not revealing the full and true state of the situation. Ben Turner, who said nothing at the meeting, later wrote in his diary: 'GC flabbergasted at nothing being settled about miners' lockout notices. Retired and felt

Stanley Baldwin speaking to journalists outside 10 Downing Street at the end of the General Strike

By permission of Mary Evans Picture Library

dismayed . . . left at 1.10 p.m. disappointed and disgusted. Papers out soon about TUC surrender.'[3]

After about an hour of discussions between the General Council and the prime minister, Neville Chamberlain emerged in a happy mood and the press representatives were let in to 10 Downing Street to hear the official announcement from both sides. Before it could be done, J.H. Thomas, clearly upset, broke away from the General Council group and crossed the road into his car. Mr Pugh then announced that the general strike had been terminated in order to facilitate the resumption of negotiations.[4] In the meantime, the BBC had announced, at 1 o'clock, that the TUC had gone to Downing Street and at 1.14 p.m. listeners were asked to stand by for a few minutes. Soon afterwards it was announced that the General Strike was at an end.

Baldwin addressed the cabinet at 2.30 that afternoon, informing them that the end of the strike was 'unconditional and immediate' and then informed the House of Commons that the dispute had ended.[5] In his speech to the House he outlined the events that led to the end of the dispute and, hoping for a resumption of negotiations in the mining industry, asked that the British people should look forward, rather than backward: 'We shall begin our work in a spirit of co-operation, putting away all malice and vindictiveness.'[6] There was not, however, any commitment to the lockout notices being withdrawn in the mines or the Samuel Memorandum.

The end of the dispute caused a flurry of activity. The government was quickly involved in meetings and most obviously met the representatives of the railway companies. Sir Arthur Steel-Maitland, minister of labour, was reported as saying that: 'He . . . wished to say that the next 48 to 72 hours would be a very critical period, and he would like the Companies to appreciate this. The Government realised the problem that had to be solved, and had made it clear that employers could not be expected to desert people who had been loyal to them. At the same time, the Railways must act on their own responsibility . . . he thought the companies should meet the Unions . . . .'[7] With 5,749 trains running, as well as 1,194 London buses on the streets, including 748 belonging to the London General Omnibus Company, it was not going to be easy for the railway and transport companies to restore relations with their unions, and one suspects from their later actions that they were not immediately inclined to restore the old terms.[8]

The problem that the government faced was alluded to in Steel-Maitland's comments to the railway companies. For several days now, the government had given guarantees that those who 'did their duty' would not be victimised after the strike. Indeed, the *British Gazette* (now with a circulation of 2,209,000) had indicated this in Baldwin's latest guarantee.

To All Workers in All Trades
Additional Guarantee
Official

Every man who does his duty by the country and remains at work or returns to work during the present crisis will be protected by the State from loss of trade union benefits, superannuation allowances, or pensions. His Majesty's Government will take whatever steps are necessary in Parliament or otherwise for this purpose.

STANLEY BALDWIN

The difficulty of this was that the government was endorsing a situation which could lead to deep conflict at the workplace and that could prove contentious in the attempt to restore relations between employers and trade unions.

The TUC, of course, also began the process of winding down the strike. The evening edition of the *British Worker* announced the termination of the strike, couched in the terms that 'the Miners will Now Get a Fair Deal'. It further indicated that telegrams had gone out to all the unions instructing them that the strike was over, for the General Council had 'reached the conclusion as a result of a number of conversations with Sir Herbert Samuel that a satisfactory basis for settlement in the mining industry can now be formulated'. The TUC Order ran as follows:

T.U.C. ORDER

In order to resume negotiations, the General Council decided to terminate the General Strike to-day.

Telegrams of instructions were sent to the Executive Committees of affiliated unions, who will communicate with the branches of their organisations, in accordance with their usual practice. Members before acting must wait definite instructions from their own Executive Councils.

The fact that this order was issued on the basis of a settlement with a leading statesman who did not represent the government, nor could commit it to anything, was skirted over by the TUC as it proceeded to publish the Samuel Memorandum. Indeed, it is clear that Samuel could not get his colleagues on the Royal Commission on Coal, much less the government, to agree to an extension of the coal subsidy. None the less, the *British Gazette* proceeded to produce the full version of the Samuel Memorandum and the TUC circulated this and various letters to its trade union organisations.[9]

The letter from Samuel to Pugh, on 12 May, reiterated that Samuel was not a government mediator: 'I have made it clear to your Committee from the outset that I have been acting entirely on my own initiative, have received no authority from the Government, and can give no assurance on their behalf.' He was, nevertheless, going to recommend the memorandum strongly to the government. Arthur Pugh replied on the same day for the TUC, accepting that the Samuel Memorandum could be a basis for the settlement of the coal crisis and stressing that the TUC had called off the strike, 'relying upon public assurances of the Prime Minister as to the steps that would follow. They assume that during the resumed negotiations the subsidy will be renewed and that the lockout notices to the Miners will be immediately withdrawn.' The Samuel Memorandum itself was much as had been first outlined on 8 May. It contained eight main points, the first and main one of which stated that: 'The negotiations upon the conditions of the coal industry should be resumed, the subsidy being renewed for such reasonable period as may be required for the purpose.' There was to be a National Wages Board, representing coal owners and coal miners, with a neutral chairman to settle disputes, and point four contained the suggestion that 'There should be no revision of the previous wage rates unless there are sufficient assurances that the measures of reorganisation proposed by the Commission will be effectively adopted.' It was, in fact, a rather neutral document although underlying it was the assumption that wages would have to be reduced while the industry reorganised. It was unrealistic of the TUC to assume that the coal miners would accept the former or that the coal owners would accept the latter. This meant that the government would be let off having to make the decision whether or not to provide a subsidy.

The General Council of the TUC was hopeful, if rather unrealistic, about the prospects for an honourable settlement in the case of the mining industry. This sense of anxiety about the final outcome, and how its decision would be received, is reflected in the fact that it needed to send out its personal message to all trade unionists, possibly in response to A.J. Cook's comment regarding the miners that 'they can be no party to the decision to call off the strike in any shape or form'. The TUC message ran as follows:

TO ALL TRADE UNIONISTS

Fellow Trade Unionists:

The General Strike has ended. It has not failed. It has secured the resumption of negotiations in the Coal Industry, and the continuance, during negotiations, of the financial assistance given by the Government.

You came out together, in accordance with the instructions of the Executive of your Unions. Return together in their instructions, as and when they are given.

Some employers will approach you as individuals with the demand that you should accept conditions different from those obtaining before the stoppage began. SIGN NO INDIVIDUAL AGREEMENT, CONSULT YOUR OWN UNION OFFICIALS AND STAND BY THEIR INSTRUCTIONS. YOUR UNION WILL PROTECT YOU AND WILL INSIST THAT ALL AGREEMENTS PREVIOUSLY IN FORCE SHALL REMAIN INTACT.

The Trade Union Movement has demonstrated its unity. That unity remains unimpaired. Stick to your unions.

FROM THE GENERAL COUNCIL

[It then continued to refer to Mr Baldwin's Sacred Promise that] our whole duty is to forget all recrimination, let employers act with generosity and workers give their whole hearts loyally to their work . . . . It is of utmost importance that the whole of the British people

should not look backward but forward and resume their work in a
spirit of co-operation and good will, putting behind them all malice
and vindictiveness.[10]

The reality is that the ending of the strike came as something of a
shock to the rank and file activists still in the throes of industrial activity.
The battle was still continuing. The Chiswick [municipal] election
resulted in a gain for Labour in a Tory stronghold, with the Labour
candidate gaining 1,041 votes while the Conservative received only 371
votes and the Liberal 133.[11] Labour leaders were still being arrested.
Alderman Jack King of Bethnal Green Borough Council was arrested
under the Emergency Powers Act and remanded for seven days on £50
bail, and Councillor A.H. Gillison was remanded late on the evening of
11 May, bail being refused. The secretary of the St Pancras Labour Party
was also arrested. Four men were arrested for an attack on food supplies
at the London docks, two men were arrested at Camden Town for
'interfering with traffic' and a special constable was arrested at Nine Elms.
Hundreds of transport workers were still picketing at Bethnal Green and
new strikers, the second line, were beginning to come out throughout
the country.[12] About 1,000 miners blocked the road with large tree
trunks in the Hatfield area of Doncaster, blocking vehicles and provoking
conflict when a large contingent of mounted police attempted to restore
order. There were seventy arrests resulting from the hand-to-hand
fighting and the stone throwing. Also, the Edenthorpe disturbances on
the Thorne Road, near Doncaster, occurred when 300 pickets blocked
the junction and attempted to stop the traffic. A detachment of police
arrived and made twelve arrests.[13]

Not surprisingly, when it was heard that the strike had been called off
there was much confusion and dismay. Miners throughout the country
greeted the decision with derision. Nevertheless, at this juncture, most of
the workers involved had come to no clear opinion about the settlement.
The flow of official announcements from Eccleston Square had seemed
to indicate victory and the theme of success was redolent within the
three editions of the *British Worker* that were produced on 12 May.

Although many of these claims were bogus it is clear that for the time
being there was confusion about what had been agreed. Also, while the
General Strike had been called off it was evident that that did not mean

an immediate return to work. None of the main unions involved permitted their members to return until they could be reasonably sure of acceptable terms of settlement. Indeed, when Bevin and his fellow General Council members returned to 10 Downing Street that evening, they were accused of calling off the strike at 12 noon and calling it on again afterwards, to which Bevin suggested that they were now exercising their constitutional right to defend their wages and agreements. But shortly afterwards the prime minister broadcast to the nation indicating that there had been no conditions entered into by the government, a statement that was to leave the General Council without the fig-leaf of the Samuel Memorandum and to leave industrial relations in something of a mess as in industry after industry strikers and management attempted to come to some accommodation.

The volunteers remained in place for the time being at a moment when their inexperience began to produce some of the most serious accidents on the railways. There was an accident when a train running from Berwick to Edinburgh, manned by a volunteer crew, crashed into a number of wagons. Three people were killed and sixteen injured. This followed a similar incident at Bishop's Stortford.[14]

Yet the dominating event of the day was the ending of the strike. What it meant was not yet clear, for it appeared that both the government and the TUC were claiming success: the government claimed to have settled the strike without any conditions while the TUC was claiming to have got the mining negotiations reopened on the basis of the Samuel Memorandum. Both the coal miners and the coal mine owners seemed unmoved. The one thing that seemed clear is that the TUC would be hesitant about calling another general strike. One London newspaper offered a fitting, if rather right-wing, epitaph to the event. 'This is the first and last General Strike that will ever take place in this country, and the probability is that when the trouble is at an end, there'll be a reorganisation of industry which will prevent any social upheaval on the present scale. If representative and constitutional Government is to continue in this country it will be the first duty of our legislature to see that individual liberty and safety are not again placed in peril.'[15]

THURSDAY 13 MAY

There were two major concerns for the TUC on 13 May. The first was that there should be no victimisation of trade unionists who were attempting to return to work. The second and related theme was that the TUC wished to establish that there were guarantees given and that the calling off of the strike was not unconditional. There was not much headway for the TUC on either issue, despite Prime Minister Baldwin's concern that there should be no victimisation, and it soon found itself under attack from the Labour Left and the communists.

The TUC issued an official bulletin which outlined what it felt the settlement meant. It indicated that it called off the strike to enable there to be a resumption of negotiations for the miners 'towards an honourable peace', and that 'Peace depends upon employers abstaining from attempts at victimisation.' The bulletin reminded its readers that the employers should 'abstain from victimisation' and further warned that the trade union movement had not been defeated and that if its members were victimised they would have no alternative but to resist: 'Their resistance capacity is unimpaired. They cannot tolerate the imposition of conditions which attempt their destruction.' It also reproduced King George V's appeal: 'Let us forget whatever elements of bitterness the events of the past few days may have created . . . and forthwith address ourselves to the task of bringing into being a peace that will be lasting because forgetting the past it looks only to the future.'[1]

The *British Worker* collaborated in this obfuscation. It stated that 'The unions that have maintained so resolutely and unitedly their generous and ungrudging support of the miners can be satisfied that an honourable understanding has been reached.'[2] Jimmy Thomas also assured the Parliamentary Labour Party that the government would honour the Samuel Memorandum.

The message was clear: the TUC had not capitulated in a moment of weakness and employers should not assume that to be the case.

Unfortunately, it was equally clear that the employers did assume weakness. On the first day after the strike this was most evident in the case of the railway companies. C.T. Cramp wrote, on behalf of the NUR, to all the railway companies explaining his union's concern.

> I wrote you yesterday to the effect that the general stoppage had been declared off and that I had advised all members of this Union to present themselves for duty. In so doing I was anxious to expedite the resumption of railway work and accomplish this in the best possible spirit.
>
> I am now receiving reports from all parts of the Country which indicate that great difficulties are being placed in the return to duty not only on the part of my own members but of railwaymen generally.
>
> I regret that this should be so and would ask you to do all in your power to remove the difficulties.
>
> If the return to the normal state of affairs in the country is to be accomplished in the spirit indicated by the Prime Minister yesterday, it would seem that the Great Railway industry can set a good example to the community in general.
>
> I am informed that a very large number of railwaymen have definitely refused to take up duty under the conditions which obtain, and it is only right that I should make it very clear that I cannot hope to influence the men to speedily take up their duties under present conditions.
>
> I should be very glad to have your early observations on the matter.[3]

As a result of this the railway companies met the railway trade unions at 6 p.m. that day. It was a difficult meeting in which Sir Felix Pole, of the GWR, suggested that when work appeared the men would be called up in terms of their seniority and he stressed that the men had broken their contract by which a month's notice would be given by either side. He added that he felt that the companies 'are legally entitled to call upon all strikers to forfeit a week's pay at normal rates. They also feel very strongly that the breach of agreement by the men should carry with it some penalty.' J. Bromley (ASLEF), representing the trade unions, said that he did not feel that there would be much complaint from the men but, referring to possible penalties, 'he did not think it possible to get the men to return with these conditions' and objected to the document which was being handed to the men to sign before reinstatement. The existence of such a document was, however, denied by Sir Felix Pole.[4] In fact, little was resolved at this meeting and it was decided to hold other meetings during the next few days, and in fact they started that afternoon.

Conscious that employers were not acting in a reasonable manner both Harold Laski and Philip Snowden, of the Labour Party, asked the prime minister to make a stand against victimisation in the House of Commons that evening. Lord Birkenhead and other hawkish members of the cabinet were hostile to such a suggestion but in the end Baldwin went his own way and stated that 'I will not countenance any attack on the part of any employers to use the present occasion for trying in any way to get reductions in wages below those in force before the strike or any increase in hours. . . . There can be no greater disaster than there should be anarchy in the trade union world.'[5] However, events suggest that Prime Minister Baldwin meant this statement more as a moral guideline than as a sign of the government's willingness to take draconian action.

Even less headway was made on the second issue, which was of great concern to the General Council. The vast majority of newspapers reported the defeat of the TUC in the General Strike. Stung by this reporting the General Council emphasised, as already indicated, that it had called off the strike from a position of strength, not weakness. It also asked the Labour Party to raise the issue of the false reporting in the House of Commons. Ramsay MacDonald met the Parliamentary Labour Party about these reports of 'unconditional surrender'. 'Accordingly, it was decided to press the Prime Minister during to-day's debate to make a statement without delay as to what his declaration of goodwill really meant in order that the declared peace might be an effective peace.'[6] In response to this challenge, Baldwin stated to the House of Commons that 'I have given no pledges at all.'[7] MacDonald responded by suggesting that he and his party would not countenance an attack upon the trade unions. This was perhaps as much in response to the BBC broadcast at 1 p.m. as to the prime minister's lack of commitment, for that broadcast committed the government to nothing.

A certificate issued by the London General Omnibus Company to a voluntary worker

By permission of the National Museum of Labour History

While it is desired that industry shall be re-established with a minimum of freedom it is pointed out that His Majesty's Government had no power to compel employers to take back men who have been on strike; they are under no obligation to do so and it must be appreciated that some displacements are inevitable in view of the reduction of business brought owing to the strike, whilst obligations are felt in many instances to volunteers who have helped to carry out the work. The hope is expressed, however, that we should resume our work in a spirit of cooperation, putting behind us all malice and vindictiveness.[8]

This, in effect, was a rewording, in a less precise form, of Baldwin's statement to the House of Commons on 12 May.

Naturally, the General Council came under intense criticism from the left of the Labour movement. The Communist Party of Great Britain issued its charges of betrayal.

The General Council's decision to call off the General Strike is the greatest crime that has ever been permitted, not only against the miners but against the working class of Great Britain and the whole world. The British workers had aroused the astonishment and admiration of the world by the enthusiasm with which they had entered upon the fight for the miners' standard of living. But instead of responding to the magnificent lead by a call to every section of organised labour to join the fight against capitalists, the General Council has miserably thrown itself and the miners on the tender mercies of the workers' worst enemies – the Tory Government.[9]

It then proceeded to note that the right wing of the General Council did not want the General Strike and that it was called off without any guarantees. The real enemy was, however, seen to be the alliance of Baldwin, Samuel and Thomas. A.J. Cook also made very similar criticisms.[10]

Despite the sweeping nature of these criticisms, they were a fairly accurate reflection of what had happened. There were no guarantees and despite the meeting between Baldwin and the miners' leaders, and between Steel-Maitland and the coal owners, it was clear that nothing was going to reopen meaningful negotiations in connection with the coal lockout.

It became obvious that the General Council had convinced itself it had been given commitments which rose above the general. It soon realised that Baldwin had hoped for an improvement in industrial relations but was not prepared to do anything to secure that improvement. As trade unionists up and down Britain came to realise, there were no guarantees and the moral authority of the government did not extend very far. Ben Tillett had informed Samuel on the eve of the end of the dispute 'We shall be told we have betrayed the miners. We will get it in the neck for sure.'[11] Tillett was right, for the recriminations began to abound, with some justification.

FRIDAY 14 MAY

It seems incredible, given the events immediately following the strike, that the *Bradford Pioneer*, the organ of the Bradford Independent Labour Party and Labour Party, should claim some type of victory from the dispute: 'We do not say the Government has been defeated by the General Strike, for it was not directed against the Government. But we do say that its object (has) been gained, and that after all the stir and excitement, the inconvenience and the lying we are back to where we wished to be, with the miners' case under negotiation.'[1] It is true that the TUC was still a potent force, which employers still needed to be cautious about, but the miners' case was scarcely under negotiation in any meaningful sense. Indeed, the focus of activity on both 13 and 14 May was the problem of getting workers back to work on the pre-strike terms. Negotiations were the order of the day and humiliation for the trade unions the normal outcome.

For many hundreds of thousands of workers there was no immediate return to work, because 'Many men who went to work were told they must accept fresh conditions and lower wages. Upon instructions from their Unions they refused to do this and were thereupon told their employers did not want them.'[2] As a result the General Council remained in permanent session and in close touch with its affiliated unions, and advised all affected trade unionists not to sign individual agreements.

When Stanley Baldwin spoke briefly in the House of Commons he noted that negotiations were going on in the transport sectors and the docks, and that work was shortly to be resumed on the buses, trams and underground railway system, although matters were still tense on the railways. 'With regard to the railways, he had received a telephone message from Mr J.H. Thomas who hoped that by the time [the premier] was making his statement a settlement would be signed between the parties which Mr Thomas believed would be satisfactory to all.'[3] Given the situation, MacDonald felt that the best thing to do was to say as little as possible.

Indeed, there were delicate negotiations going on. They were agreed at a conference that lasted several hours between the representatives of the three major unions and the railway managers. The final terms of the agreement are indicated below.

(1) Those employees of the railway companies who have gone out on strike to be taken back to work as soon as traffic officers and work can be found for them. The principle to be followed in re-instating to be seniority in each grade at each station, depot, or office.

(2) The trade unions admit that in calling a strike they committed a wrongful act against the companies and agree that the companies do not by reinstatement surrender their legal right to claims/damages arising out of the strike from strikers and others responsible.

(3) The unions undertake (a) not again to instruct their members to strike without previous negotiation with the company; (b) to give no support of any kind to their members to take any unauthorised action; (c) not to encourage supervisory employees in the special class to take part in any strike.

(4) The companies intimate that, arising out of the strike it may be necessary to remove certain persons to other positions, but no such persons' salaries or wages will be reduced. Each company will notify the union within one week of the names of men whom they propose to transfer, and will afford each man an opportunity of having an advocate to present his case to the General Manager.

(5) The settlement shall not extend to persons who have been guilty of violence or intimidation.

Signed on behalf of the General Managers' Conference: Felix J.C. Pole, H.G. Burgess, H.A. Walker, R.I. Wedgewood, R.H. Selbie.

On behalf of the Railway Unions: J.H. Thomas and C.T. Cramp (National Union of Railwaymen), J. Bromley (Associated Society of Locomotive Engineers and Firemen), A.G. Walkden (Railway Clerks' Association).

Mr J.H. Thomas, in a statement to the press at the conclusion of the conference after signing the agreement said:

'Having regard to all the circumstances I consider it an eminently satisfactory settlement. When one considers the bitterness, the disorganisation and the difficulties surrounding the whole situation, I hope that the men will accept it in the spirit in which the companies and the leaders signed the agreement, namely a genuine desire to do all that is humanly possible immediately to restart the wheels of industry.'

Mr Bromley, secretary of the Associated Society of Locomotive Engineers and Firemen, said: 'Those who, like myself, know all the difficulties with which they were at first confronted in negotiating for a settlement will, I am sure, feel as I do, that finally a very satisfactory arrangement has been arrived at. Naturally, when the first position of the railway companies following the end of the General Strike was known, my members solidly refused to return to duty, and a similar action was taken by the other unions. I feel now that my members generally will accept the position and work will be resumed and carried on smoothly.'

Mr Walkden, secretary of the Railway Clerks' Association, said that '. . . he felt that the settlement would prove satisfactory'.[4]

Indeed, there was much optimism that the railway strike was settled. The main concern of the railway unions had been that, as the NUR put it, 'none of our members should sign any form of re-engagement'.[5] That objective had been achieved and it was felt that the terms, humiliating as they were, if adhered to would provide a suitable settlement. The men were to return to work the following day. These terms of settlement, however, did not necessarily meet with the demands of the 30,000 railwaymen who had marched through Manchester that day, and the many thousands of others throughout the country who had done the same, demanding unconditional reinstatement.

Other groups of workers had also settled with their employers. The London Underground workers and management came to an agreement and it was hoped that there would be a normal service on 15 May.[6] The agreement allowed for the reinstatement of all the men, but not necessarily to their former posts, and some might have to accept inferior positions. It was also accepted that those who had volunteered to keep on working throughout the dispute would not be interfered with.[7] However, elsewhere there was still some concern that employers were attempting to impose non-unionism and reduce wages and that workers should not accept any terms until they received instructions from their unions.[8]

Other than such agreements, the only other significant development of the day was that the government published its disclaimer of the Samuel Memorandum and outlined its own proposal for a settlement in the coal dispute, based on compulsory arbitration agreed by a wages board, with a temporary wage reduction, the restructuring of the coal industry and a temporary subsidy to ease the wage cuts. It was estimated that the subsidy would cost about £3 million to the government, which still meant that there would be wage cuts of about 10 per cent.[9]

Some progress had been made at getting the workers to return to work but there were many occupational groups who were still out on strike, resisting the attempt of employers to worsen their conditions. There was also uncertainty about how matters would work out within those occupational groups that had settled with the demeaning terms agreed.

Arthur Pugh leaving Downing Street

By permission of the Illustrated London News *Picture Library*

SATURDAY TO FRIDAY
15–21 MAY

From 15 May to the end of the following week there were three main developments in the process of returning to normality. The first was a tendency for newspapers to reflect upon the strike, to publish photographs of the events and to urge that such an event had to be avoided in the future. The second was that the TUC attempted to boost its position and to limit the damage that the ending of the strike had created. Thirdly, there was the attempt by the trade unions to get their members back to work on acceptable, if humiliating, terms. The government and the authorities were on the offensive and the trade unions were fighting an important rearguard action.

From 15 May most newspapers were getting back to full production and took the opportunity to produce reports on the General Strike illustrated with pictures of the derailment of the 'Flying Scotsman' and the work of the volunteers. Indeed, there were even photographs of the 'Dover Fifty' at work.[1] *The Sphere* and the *Illustrated London News* began to publish many of the photographs of the General Strike with which we are now familiar. The historical record was being built up, with the emphasis on the reasonableness of the authorities and the unprincipled, unconstitutional and unnecessary actions of the trade unions.

The trade union movement was necessarily defensive. Indeed, the TUC published the following note on 15 May to attempt to cement unity with its trade unionists and rank and file members.

THANKS OF THE GENERAL COUNCIL

The General Council desires to tender its sincere thanks to the very large number of members of the Labour Movement and sympathisers who readily and freely placed their services at the disposal of the Trade Union Movement during the recent stoppage.

The General Council cannot thank them all individually, as there are so many, and accordingly they are asked to accept collective thanks.

The response for assistance was wonderful – whether in connection with transport, publicity, the production and distribution of the BRITISH WORKER, despatch carrying, clerical work or the various other sections of strike activity.

This voluntary service is highly appreciated, and the General Council desires to place on record its grateful thanks to all who have assisted in the splendid demonstration of working class unity and solidity on behalf of the locked-out Mineworkers.

ARTHUR PUGH (Chairman)
WALTER CITRINE (Acting Secretary)

May 15, 1926[2]

Yet such stirring words did not protect trade unionists from the harsh reality of having to negotiate the best terms available to get their jobs back. On 15 May the General Printing Trades came to an accommodation with their workers. Signed by A. Goodwin, the secretary of the Printing and Kindred Trades' Federation, it was a six-point agreement which re-engaged the men as and when required, accepted the need to work short time in order to get as many former employees as possible re-employed, and allowed no holidays to those who had left work without notice.[3]

On 16 May the Bradford Dyers' Association declared that, notwithstanding the return to work, it would take legal action against the Amalgamated Society of Dyers to enforce its right under the Agreement of 1 July 1914, relating to the breaches of contract committed by the trade unionists. It was also going to claim £1 from every workman who had left work.[4]

Two other settlements were made on 16 May. The Printing Machine Managers' Trades Society instructed its members to resume work.[5] The London newspaper workers also accepted a seven-point agreement which deprived them of many rights. They accepted that 'There shall be no interference with the control of the newspapers owned by members of the association', that there would be no victimisation of the volunteers, that management would be allowed to employ or discharge members of staff as they wished, and that 'No chapel meetings shall be held during working hours'. The main innovation, however, was that 'There shall be a joint committee of three from each side, which shall sit each day at three o'clock, to decide any cases which may rise. . . .' The 50,000 men working at the London docks also accepted the employers' terms, accepted that they had broken their contracts and agreed not to strike again without following the arrangements in the National Agreement.[6] Ernest Bevin stated that 'These terms in London are acceptable to the Union' and suggested that they could be the basis of a settlement at other ports.

Nevertheless, there were still problems in many other areas of the country. In Hull, for instance, there were still more than 30,000 railwaymen, printers, engineers and dockers on strike in support of the reinstatement of about 150 tramway employees. In Eastbourne, members of all trades were still protesting against the victimisation of tramwaymen.

There were numerous other agreements as well.[7] They were not easy to accept or operate and the railway unions quickly complained that their agreement was not being implemented by the employers. On 20 May Mr Cramp of the NUR informed the railway companies that they had broken the agreement of 14 May by failing to reinstate supervisors and clerical staff, continuing to employ volunteers, and continuing to let some men work overtime while others were awaiting re-employment.[8] Indeed, on 21 May the railway unions had to swallow another bitter pill when they lost the guaranteed working week for their members.[9] Then two sides met again on the following day, 2 June and 2 July to raise similar issues.[10]

The meeting on 2 July included a report from C.T. Cramp that:

In practice, however, removals are not only being carried out . . . but men are being removed and reduced in status, which they allege is directly contrary to the terms of the Settlement, and no mention of status was ever made during the negotiations. Inspectors at Edinburgh have been transferred to posts of Signalman and Guard representing a transfer from Salaried to Wages status never contemplated.

A Chief Inspector at York has been reduced to the position of Assistant Inspector at another place although beyond the fact that he went on strike, there is nothing whatever against him.

There is no doubt that the contracts broken by the workers who left work without notice at the beginning of the General Strike continued to present problems for some time afterwards. The employers sought to gain advantage and the workers sought to prevent victimisation. Indeed, in the end about 1,900 busmen and transport workers alone lost their jobs.[11] Many others, in different occupations, also lost their jobs or were victimised. The unions faced having to accept humiliating terms in order to get their men back to work. Yet for all this suffering and commitment nothing had been resolved as far the coal mining industry was concerned. The coal dispute continued even as the problems caused by the General Strike were being resolved and did not come to an end until November 1926.

How the nation was kept informed: reading the Wireless Bulletins at Marconi House, London
By permission of the Illustrated London News *Picture Library*

THE RECKONING

Clearly, the end of the General Strike did not bring about a settlement to the coal crisis which had provoked it; it also opened up a debate and criticism about the actions taken by the General Council. Neither situation was flattering to the credibility of the British trade union movement, and both provoked an attempt at damage limitation and redirected trade union opinions towards working for political solutions for their concerns.

For the coal industry there was to be no solution to the lockout which continued from the end of April until November 1926. Both the coal miners and the coal owners remained intractable. Herbert Smith was opposed to a settlement which did not protect the wages and conditions of the miners while Cook began to favour compromise. Indeed, Cook did enter secret negotiations with Seebohm Rowntree and Sir Stephen Demetriadi, the chairman of London Chamber of Commerce, towards the end of July. The emphasis of these negotiations was placed on an acceptance of some version of the Samuel Commission Report but neither set of negotiations got anywhere and remained 'covert single-handed negotiations', of which the MFGB knew nothing until 1928.[1]

As already indicated, there had been earlier attempts to settle the dispute. Baldwin had met the coal miners on 13 May and Steel-Maitland met the coal owners on 14 May, but neither meeting had produced much encouragement for industrial peace. On 14 May the government had outlined its proposals for compulsory arbitration and a temporary subsidy, but again that proposal got nowhere and the Miners' Special Conference rejected the suggestion on 20 May.[2] The mine owners also rejected the government proposals. At this point the government effectively withdrew from negotiations, although Baldwin did meet the miners and Bevin at the end of May when he urged them to accept longer hours: 'Put it to them that "hours" was the way out. If they went on with the strike they would be beaten. I did not move them.'[3]

Convinced that the raising of working hours was the way out of the dispute, the government decided to suspend the Seven Hours Act for five years on 15 June 1926, and enacted this decision on 8 July, accompanied by a Mining Industry Act which implemented the measures for reorganisation, when the Eight Hours Bill received Royal Assent.[4] Within four days the coal owners had posted up fresh wage rates, the result of which meant wage cuts in most districts. These actions united the TUC and the MFGB, which might otherwise have been embroiled in internecine conflict as a result of A.J. Cook's recently published pamphlet *The Nine Days*.

There were numerous, if limited, attempts to bring the coal dispute to a close. On 30 July a delegate conference of the miners endorsed what has become known as the Bishops' Memorandum, which advocated aspects of the Samuel Report including wage cuts, but this effort was thwarted by the fact that on 19 July Baldwin had already announced that he would not consider providing a further subsidy. In any case, when the miners voted on the matter the proposal was rejected by a narrow majority of 34,000.

The miners later revealed their willingness to compromise when a delegate conference held on 17 August allowed the executive to reopen negotiations with the coal owners and the government without conditions. However, the coal owners took this as a sign of weakness and made it clear that they would accept nothing less than total surrender at their meeting with the miners' executive on 19 August. Herbert Smith replied by suggesting that the miners had made a reasonable offer and, in a dramatic flourish, announced that 'A fair deal I will put up with, but I will not have it crammed down me – that I will resist. Good afternoon.'[5]

The miners' executive contacted the government again on 24 August but got nowhere. Thereafter, it was not until 2 September, when a miners' delegate conference instructed the executive to prepare proposals for a settlement, that the miners began to look seriously for a settlement. The initiative led to a flurry of activities at Sir Abe Bailey's house in Bryanstan Square on 3 September between Churchill, MacDonald and the miners' officials which led to a formula for a 'new national agreement with a view to a reduction of labour costs'.[6] Immediately, Churchill and the cabinet's Coal Committee pursued this possibility but met the Mining Association which refused to consider any such national arrangement, especially since they felt that they were close to victory and that district agreements would be imposed. There were several weeks of inconsequential negotiations before the cabinet eventually put forward a plan, drafted by Cunliffe-Lister, to establish a wage tribunal with the power to revise, on appeal, district agreements on an eight-hour basis. However, this was also rejected by the coal owners and by the miners, with a majority of almost 700,000.[7]

During the next few weeks there was a complex array of posturing going on, with the miners reasserting their original position and the General Council attempting to enter the dispute. Yet they were faced with the cabinet Coal Committee's decision to support district negotiations covering hours and wages. These proposals were rejected by 460,806 to 313,200 votes when put to the miners.[8] The MFGB therefore ordered its various regions to make their own terms consistent, as far as possible, with the agreed national standards. From then onwards the miners in various regions began to drift back to work on varied terms and most of the coalfields were working again by the end of November. All the workers returned on a $7\frac{1}{2}$ hour day in Yorkshire, while longer hours and wage reductions were imposed in South Wales, Scotland and the North-East. In Nottinghamshire, those workers who had returned to work under George Spencer's breakaway union were given a four shilling per week wage increase.

After almost seven months of heroic struggle the miners had been forced to capitulate. They and their families had been starved into submission, supported only by the minimal contribution of a levy from the TUC-affiliated trade unions and with some financial support from the Soviet Union. In this state of affairs, the General Council of the TUC attempted to put the best gloss on a bad situation.

This was not easy, especially when the TUC decided not to support a boycott of imported coal. Nevertheless, in return for the support of the TUC, the miners held their fire and even Cook's pamphlet *The Nine Days* was subject to some constraint. There was, indeed, almost a conspiracy of silence with occasional outbursts of feeling, as at the TUC Conference held at Bournemouth between 6 and 11 September 1926. Ultimately, however, the General Council was subject to a variety of charges – including its unwillingness to prepare for the strike, its failure to protect the workers from victimisation and its ending of the strike without any guarantees – which it was to rebut at a Conference of the Trade Union Executives on 20 and 21 January 1927. Its main defence was that if the miners had accepted the Samuel Memorandum the government would have had to accept it as a basis for compromise.[9] This was an argument that was hardly likely to satisfy the Labour Left and the communists, and it seems highly unlikely that the government could ever have accepted the Samuel Memorandum given the stand it had taken towards the end of the dispute. In the end, the General Council failed to acquit itself of the charge of betrayal.

For the next few years, as before the General Strike, the level of industrial conflict in Britain began to fall. In this period the trade unions seemed to have given their increasing support to political action, especially after the industrial restrictions imposed by the Trades Dispute Act of 1927. It was an increasingly contentious alliance but did help to bring about the return of the Labour government of 1929. But even this fleeting political victory did not wash away the fact that the miners had been badly let down nor that the General Council had failed to commit itself wholeheartedly to the General Strike.

CONCLUSION

The debates about the causes, events and consequences of the General Strike have already been examined in the introductory chapter and it is not the purpose here to reiterate these issues. Rather, the intent is to assess what the daily record of the General Strike indicates about the participants and their motivation and performance. In these terms the dominant themes have to be the limited commitment of the General Council and the resolute and determined action of the government not to negotiate under duress nor to permit the trade unions to control the situation.

The General Council of the TUC clung to one desire throughout the dispute and that was to gain a settlement based upon the Samuel Report, which provided the basis for the Samuel Memorandum. It was this report which formed the basis of its approach on the eve of the dispute and throughout. In choosing to negotiate with Samuel from 7 May onwards it was further committing itself to a strategy which would contain some of the recommendations of the Samuel Report. Yet the one thing that was obvious throughout is that the MFGB would not accept any terms which reduced wages, lengthened hours or, as became important later, involved national agreements. In the end, the miners preferred to negotiate *ad hoc* district agreements rather than come to some humiliating national agreement with the mine owners.

The confusion that arose when the strike was called off was partly due to the belief of the General Council that the Samuel negotiations could lead to a settlement, but also to the fact that Jimmy Thomas deliberately kept the General Council in the dark about the precise relationship of Samuel to the government and misled Samuel, from time to time, about the willingness of the miners to accept the terms. Thomas's lack of commitment to the strike is legendary and became evident throughout the nine days, although his own union (the NUR) overruled his opposition to strikes from the outset and performed impressively in bringing the railways to a halt.

One might also note that the mood of the General Council changed dramatically from one of organising the strike to one of negotiating a settlement from 7 May onwards – with or without the consent of the miners. Once a settlement of some description was in sight the focus of the General Council's activities was placed on the Samuel negotiations.

Yet, notwithstanding its lukewarm commitment to the strike, it is obvious that the General Council did achieve some successes. The strike was effective at the local level, despite confusion between the councils of action and the trades councils about their duties. The railways were brought to an effective halt and even the efforts of managers and volunteers did not make tremendously significant inroads into the railway stoppages. The London docks, and other dock areas, were closed down in the early days of the dispute. In effect, the General Council was organising the most obvious and significant episode of class conflict in modern British history. The strike was supported and operated by millions of working people but not supported by the vast majority of the middle classes who saw it as their duty to volunteer or support the government. The stark contrast could be overdone, with an undue emphasis being placed on student volunteers, the 'plus-four brigade' and the like, but as near as one could get this was a situation of intense class conflict. It was a situation, of course, which the General Council was unwilling and unable to handle.

The government in contrast was committed to the line it took and unwilling to negotiate until the strike was called off. It worked with the OMS, appealed for volunteers to work the railways and docks and for those who were willing to join the specials. It realised that its ability to keep the railways going was limited but recognised that its great need was to control the movement of food and supplies. To this end it decided by 8 May that the effective blockade of the London docks had to be broken. It was equally determined that it, and it alone, would have control of the airwaves. It did not prevent the TUC from producing a newspaper, although it interrupted its production from time to time and confiscated some of its newsprint supplies. Its own newspaper, the *British Gazette*, was one of the most blatantly propagandist newspapers ever produced.

Though aware that the General Council had no stomach for a major conflict and had no revolutionary intentions in mind, the Conservative government also played the constitutional card for all it was worth. It had prepared for the worst, reflected that the strike threatened the British Constitution and discussed the possibility of pushing a bill through Parliament at top speed to ban sympathetic strike action. Yet it soon became clear that the General Council had no heart for the matter and was busily working towards a settlement. Even at the end of the dispute, there was nothing more for the government to do except hope that a return to work would be achieved without too many disturbances or too much victimisation. But its position was somewhat vague and moralistic. It wished to protect the interests of those who had done their duty to the nation during the strike, and acknowledged that it had little power to force the employers to avoid victimisation even though there was the moral commitment of Baldwin to opposing victimisation. However, the government's moral edict did not extend far and, given the strength of opposition to a settlement by the mine owners, it is perhaps not surprising that it was never able to open effective negotiations to settle the coal lockout or to avoid continuing disturbances on the railways.

In the final analysis, the General Strike revealed the real weakness of a constitutional trade union movement supporting a course of action to which it was reluctantly committed and whose consequences would have had to be measured in political as well as industrial terms. In effect the General Council, doubting its own ability to sustain the General Strike, convinced itself of the need for industrial peace and forced a resolute government to do little other than attempt to maintain the movement of vital food supplies until the conflict was called off. The General Strike was therefore a landmark in British history, for it revealed to the General Council the limits of its own industrial policy in the face of a powerful and committed government.

Selected Documents

Document 1

General Council of the TUC 'proposal for co-ordinated action, put to the trade unions on 30 April and adopted 1 May', TUC General Council, *The Mining Crisis and the National Strike* (London, TUC, June 1926, p. 32 A)

1. SCOPE

The Trades Union Congress General Council and the Miners' Federation of Great Britain having been unable to obtain a satisfactory settlement of the matters in dispute in the coalmining industry, and the Government and the mineowners having forced a lockout, the General Council, in view of the need for co-ordinated action on the part of the affiliated unions in defence of the policy laid down by the General Council of the Trades Union Congress directs as follows:

TRADES AND UNDERTAKINGS TO CEASE WORK
Except as hereinafter provided, the following trades and undertakings shall cease work as and when required by the General Council:

Transport, including all affiliated unions connected with Transport i.e. railways, sea transport . . . .

Printing trades, including the Press.

Productive industries. (a) Iron and steel. (b) Metal and Heavy Chemical Group. Including all metal workers and other workers who are engaged, or may be engaged, in installing alternative plant to take the place of coal.

Building trade. All workers engaged on building, except such as are employed definitely in housing and hospital work . . . shall cease work.

Electricity and gas . . . Trade unions connected with the supply of electricity and gas shall co-operate with the object of ceasing to supply power. The Council request that the Executives of the Trade Unions concerned shall meet at once with a view to formulating common policy.

Sanitary services. The General Council direct that sanitary services be continued.

Health and food services. The General Council recommend that there should be no interference in regard to these, and that the Trade Union concerned should do everything in their power to organize the distribution of milk and food for the whole population.

With regard to hospitals, clinics, convalescent homes, sanatoria, infant welfare centres, maternity homes, nursing homes, schools, the General Council direct that every affiliated union take every opportunity to ensure that food, milk, medical and surgical supplies shall be efficiently provided.

2. TRADE UNION DISCIPLINE

. . . (b) The General Council recommend that the actual calling out of the workers shall be left to the unions, and instructions should only be issued by the accredited representatives of the unions participating in the dispute.

3. TRADES COUNCILS

The work of the Trades Councils, in conjunction with the local officers of the trade unions actually participating in the dispute, shall be to assist in carrying out the foregoing provisions (i.e. stoppage of work in various trades and undertakings, and the exceptions thereto), and they shall be charged with the responsibility of organising the trade unionists in dispute in the most effective manner for the preservation of peace and orders.

4. . . .

5. . . .

6. PROCEDURES

(a) These proposals shall be immediately considered by the Executive of the Trade Unions concerned in the stoppage, who will at once report as to whether they will place their powers in the hands of the General Council and carry out the instructions which the General Council may issue from time to time concerning the necessary action and the conduct of the dispute.

(b) And, further, that the Executive of all other affiliated unions are asked to report at once as to whether they will place their powers in the hands of the General Council and carry out the instructions of the General Council from time to time, both regarding the conduct of the dispute and financial assistance.

A. Pugh, Chairman

Walter M. Citrine, Acting Secretary

Document 2

The General Strike: Extracts from Speech by the Prime Minister and Mr Winston Churchill, House of Commons May 3rd 1926 (London, HMSO, 1926), pp. 3–10; *Hansard*, 3 May 1926

[The General Council had taken over the responsibility for the General Strike.]

THREAT OF GENERAL STRIKE

It was not an easy position for the Government to know what was the right and wise thing to do, but I decided that I would ask them to come and see me at once, that I would ignore the threat for the moment, so anxious was I to see if even at the last moment we might find a way out of the position which had become almost insoluble . . . .

After a time, I felt that the large body that we had then . . . was far too formidable a body to make progress. I suggested that they should just have three of their body and I would have two colleagues and a permanent official. That was done and we sat up between 1 and 2 on Sunday morning.

AN ASSURANCE WANTED

I and those who were negotiating with me . . . wanted to get to a position where we could get an assurance that the Trades Union Council, on behalf of the miners, would say that they really believed, the phrase I used was that they felt confident, that given a fortnight, the time I named, a settlement would be arrived at on the basis of the Report.

At the last moment I and my colleagues, if we could have got that complete assurance, would have risked it; we would have asked for another fortnight, and, I think, if necessary, we would have paid for another fortnight. But it is no good going on with the experience we had had for the past fortnight, in any negotiations unless we could have some assurance that there was a reasonable hope of success.

It would have been a pure waste of time if we had got back to the same deadlock. That was what was felt at the time. We strove manfully and honestly for it.

MINERS RE-CALLED

When we parted early on Sunday morning, the three who had been consulting with us, were going to see the miners that morning later, and they hoped to be in a position to let us know whether they had the miners' endorsement by about 12 or 1, or it might be rather later. They were going to see them first thing.

I summoned the cabinet at 12 o'clock on the chance of the answer coming earlier, but when it did not come through then – there is no charge of bad faith – we met later in the afternoon to get the answer. But those who were negotiating with me found to their great surprise that the miners had left London, and so they were unable to get in touch with them. In that way a great deal of Sunday was lost. But so anxious were they to get to business that they re-called the miners to London that night.

About 9 o'clock on Sunday night, when we resumed discussions, we made another effort to see whether it was possible to obtain the sort of assurance which we, on behalf of the Government, felt was essential if we were to comply with the request for further time – namely, an assurance that there would be an acceptance of the Report.

In this expression, 'acceptance of the Report', is included both the reorganisation of the industry, which was to be put in hand immediately, and, pending the results of reorganisation being attained, such interim adjustment of wages and hours of work as would make it economically possible to carry on the industry in the meantime . . . .

STRIKE INSTRUCTIONS ISSUED

It had come to our knowledge during Sunday afternoon – that is to my knowledge – that specific instructions had already gone out under the authority of the executives of the trade unions represented at the conference directing their members in several of the most vital industries of the country to carry out a general strike to-morrow.

That had, of course, moved it on a very considerable stage from where it was on Saturday. My position was becoming an increasingly difficult one. Yet, with that knowledge, I continued those negotiations on the Sunday evening, and I ran what every one who visualises my position will see was a real risk.

But while the parties with whom I was in discussion last night left the room for consultation, and I went to consult my colleagues at 11.30, I learned that certain overt acts had already taken place in anticipation of the general strike, acts, perhaps, not so great in themselves, but great in their possible consequences, and certainly in their signification. Those were acts interfering with the freedom of the Press.

Such actions as that, coupled with the notice that we had had of instructions sent out by the representative leaders of the unions, instructions which men could only carry out in many cases by breaking their contracts, made me realise that I had got to the point where it would be impossible for the Government, or for me to persuade the Government, to pursue these negotiations any further . . . .

NEAR TO CIVIL WAR

I do not think all the leaders who assented to order a general strike full realised that they were threatening the basis of ordered government and coming nearer to proclaiming civil war than we have been for centuries past. They have laboured, that is many of them, with the utmost zeal for peace up to the very end.

Perhaps they thought that there was nothing more at stake than bringing a certain amount of spectacular pressure to bear which might suffice to persuade the Government to capitulate without serious damage to the liberties of the nation, but they have created a machine they cannot control. I tried to co-operate with Mr Pugh and his colleagues in the search for an agreement to the last possible moment, but I became convinced last night (Sunday) that Mr Pugh and those with him who sought peace were not in control of the situation, and that it would be wrong and dangerous for the Government to continue talking unless we got an immediate and unconditional withdrawal of the instructions for the general strike . . . .

Document 3

This is a short extract of the reflections of Jack Dash, a docker of more recent years, recording his experiences of the General Strike and related in *Nine Days 1926: The General Strike in Southwark* (London, Union Place Community Resource Centre, 1976), pp. 28–9

There were tremendous battles in the streets of Southwark. The young people, Jack included, would wait on the roofs of tenement buildings along the New Kent Road for an opportunity to rain stones and bottles down on the heads of the specials . . . . The police would respond with waves of violence: there were ugly scenes every day, especially around the Bricklayers' Arms where dockers and railwaymen gathered. . . .

One day Jack went over London Bridge with his mates and saw the tanks, the armoured cars and the Scots troopers gathering at the Bank: this had a powerful effect on the young people. 'In retrospect, I can see now that it was a great lesson. It was a revolutionary situation and good political education.' Then suddenly the strike was ended. Jack's dad called the Congress of the TUC 'traitorous bastards', as did many others. Nearly everyone was sorry it was over. 'The Railway Class learned a lot from the strike – there are now more knights around the table than there ever were around King Arthur's.'

Document 4

PRO, RAIL 786, 6, Chief of Police Daily Report for the Great Western Railway, 8 May 1926

Special Constables enrolled up to date

Paddington	557	Acton	18	Ealing	18	Southwark	19
Slough	47	Reading	26	Didcot	19	Swindon	16
Trowbridge	3	Weymouth	25	Bristol	55	Taunton	17

Exeter	24	N. Abbot	22	Plymouth	31	Gloucester	15
Newport	76	Cardiff	218	P. Talbot	40	Neath	18
Swansea	34	Llanelly	28	Carmarthen	20	Aberdare	9
Pontypool Rd	20	Severn T.W.	20	Pontypridd	23	Caerphilly	18
Bangor	12	Merthyr	10	Worcester	34	Hereford	10
Banbury	20	Birmingham	68	Stansbridge J.	30	Shrewsbury	20
Oswestry	51	Chester	12	Birkenhead	55		
Wolverhampton	112						

Total 1,869

Document 5

The BBC broadcast of Prime Minister Baldwin, Saturday 8 May 1926, as reported in the *Daily Express*, 10 May 1926

What is the issue for which the Government is fighting? It is fighting because while the negotiations were still in progress the TUC ordered a general strike, presumably to force Parliament and the community to heed its will.

With that object the TUC has declared that the railways shall not move and that the unloading of ships shall stop, and that no news shall reach the public. The supply of electricity, the transportation of food supplies of the people have been interrupted.

The TUC declare that this is merely an industrial dispute, but their method of helping the miners is to affect the community.

Can there be a more direct attack upon the community than that a body not elected by the voters of the country, without consulting even trade unionists, and in order to impose conditions never yet defined should disrupt the life of the nation and try to starve it into submission?

I wish to make it as clear as I can that the Government is not fighting to lower the standard of living of the miners or any other class of workers.

My whole desire is to maintain the standard of living of every worker, and I am ready to press the employers to make every sacrifice to this end, consistent with keeping industry in its proper working order.

This is the Government's position. The general strike must be called off absolutely and without reserve. The mining dispute can then be settled . . . .

I am a man of peace. I am longing and working and praying for peace,

But I will not surrender the safety and security of the British Constitution.

You have placed me in power eighteen months ago by the largest majority afforded to any party for many years.

Have I done anything to forfeit that confidence? Cannot you trust me to ensure a square deal for the parties and secure even justice between man and man?

Document 6

The TUC, 'Where We Stand', *British Worker*, 10 May 1926

WHERE WE STAND

It is being persistently stated that Mr Ramsay MacDonald, Mr Herbert Samuel, Mr Arthur Cook and other Trade Union leaders have been engaged in an attempt to re-open negotiations with a view to ending the General Stoppage.

The General Council wish it to be clearly understood that there is no truth in this assertion.

No official or unofficial overtures have been made to the Government by any individual or group of individuals, either with or without the sanction of the General Council. Complete control of all negotiations is vested in the General Council, who have had no direct communication with the Government since they sent their emphatic letter of protest against the cabinet's wanton action in wrecking the peace discussions that were proceeding.

The position of the General Council may be stated in simple and unequivocal terms. They are ready at a moment to enter into preliminary discussions regarding the withdrawal of the lockout notices and ending in the General Stoppages and the resumption of negotiations for an honourable settlement of the Mining Dispute. These preliminary discussions must be free from any condition.

The Government must remember, and the public are asked to remember, that the General Stoppages took place as a result of the action of the cabinet in breaking off peace discussions and issuing their ultimatum, using as their excuse the unauthorized action of the printing staff of a London newspaper. The responsibility of the present grave situation rests entirely upon the cabinet. Even the newspapers concerned admit it to be true 'that when the negotiations broke down the trade union representatives knew nothing of the stoppage of the *Daily Mail*'.

It is therefore merely fantastic for the Prime Minister to pretend that the Trade Unions are engaged in an attack upon the Constitution of the Country. Every instruction issued by the General Council is evidence of their determination to maintain the struggle strictly on the basis of an industrial dispute. They have ordered every member taking part to be exemplary in his conduct and not to give any cause for police interference.

The General Council struggled hard for peace. They are anxious that an honourable peace shall be secured as soon as possible.

They are not attacking the Constitution. They are fighting the community. They are defending the mine workers against the mine owners.

Document 7

Here are extracts taken from the National Union of Railwaymen, *General Strike News Bulletin*, 11 May 1926, a copy of which is in the National Museum of Labour History, NMLH/GS/SCB/006. It begins with an appeal, from C.T. Cramp, for union members to remain steadfast, then lists brief reports from 116 centres and includes parts of a speech by J.H. Thomas and by C.T. Cramp.

TO THE BRANCH AND STRIKE
COMMITTEE SECRETARIES
GENERAL STRIKE NEWS BULLETIN
TUESDAY, 11 MAY 1926

A telegraphic message in the following terms was circulated to all Branches and Strike Committees this morning.

EVERYTHING GOING WELL IN SPITE OF ALL ATTEMPTS TO MISLEAD. IGNORE ANY INSTRUCTIONS OTHER THAN FROM THIS OFFICE. REMAIN SOLID. ALL OUR MEMBERS WILL RESOLUTELY REFUSE TO BE ASSOCIATED WITH ANY ACTS OF WRECKAGE AND DESTRUCTION.

We have now entered on the second week of the Strike, and we are stronger today than ever we were; stronger not only by experience of the loyalty of our members, but by the fact that not a single instance of deviation by any centre can be found.

The reports that so many thousands of Railwaymen are at work should be entirely ignored. Those who are at work belong to the Administrative Staff and not to the Rank and File. Those who belong to the Railway Trade Unions have ceased work practically to a man, and can be relied on to remain solid to the end, notwithstanding the efforts being made by the Railway Companies to induce the men to return to work. Personal letters have been addressed to members of staff, and these have, in a number of instances, been followed up by telegrams of mysterious origin, instructing them to report for duty at a certain time. This indicates the efforts being made to mislead our men.

Rumours have also been circulated to the effect that no members of the Supervisory and Clerical Staffs will be reinstated until sanctioned by the General Manager. This is obviously another attempt to mislead the men and coerce them to return to work. IT CANNOT BE TOO STRONGLY EMPHASISED THAT THESE RUMOURS SHOULD BE TREATED WITH THE CONTEMPT THEY DESERVE.

THE FORCES AGAINST YOU ARE DISPLAYING WEAKNESS BY THESE INSIDIOUS ATTEMPTS TO DECEIVE. IGNORE THEM, AND REMAIN FIRM AND LOYAL TO YOUR UNIONS.

'KEEP STEADFAST'

C.T. CRAMP (Signed)

Branch	Nature of Letter or Telegram
Slades Green	All solid.
Merthyr Tydfil	Position very firm – complete stoppage.
Cudworth	Still firm and in good heart
Immingham	We are O.K. here.
Wymondham	Solidarity maintained
South Milford	Position firmer than ever. Members solid.
Halifax	Position unchanged – position solid. Unparalleled enthusiasm.

Branch	Nature of Letter or Telegram
Manchester	Manchester 12 maintaining 100% solidarity.
Tyne Dock 1	Stoppage 100%.
Garforth	Every member of branch out.
Newport (Mon.)	All solid and quiet.
Wakefield	All men standing firm.
Kettering	All out.
Barnsley	All Unions solid.
Nottingham	Firm as a rock in this district.
Rochdale	Position unchanged, including Bury 2 – solid.
Leeds 6, 10, 11, 12 & 15	NUR Associated and RCA out to a man.
Middlesbrough	Position solid – all standing firm – splendid conduct of our men.
Aviemore	All firm – none gone back.
Battersea 3	All solid.
Lancaster	Position solid.
Blackburn	Men standing firm – all working together. Central strike committee composed of all Unions involved.
Oxford	Going well – All out – Clarendon Press 100% out.
Wrexham	All Union combined – solid – complete blockage.

Speaking at Stoke Newington, Mr Cramp said:

. . . I know how feeling runs high. I know how difficult it is always to control oneself when one sees how things are happening that are calculated to provoke tempers to an extraordinary degree. Never mind all that. Let your pickets display their badges quite prominently so that no one can mistake them. Let no excuse be given to those who would provoke disorder, because, ultimately disorder spells disorganisation. Those of you who are not pickets yourselves or are not on duty as pickets keep right away from the place of duty and get out and get fresh air; play with your children, keep away from the scene of operations. I feel this to be a responsibility not merely to the men I represent, but also a responsibility to their Wives and children. I would have nothing happen which, when this is finished, can inflict sorrow on any home in this Country. . . .

Remember in this fight that while the Miners are the immediate persons who we are trying to help the fight is ultimately a fight for the whole of the Workers of this Country. We established a principle last July which said that there is a point below which you must not force down any human being in this Country. Just as we established it then we are fighting to maintain it now. If the miners were forced down it would ultimately mean that every Worker, in every Country, would find it more difficult to resist reductions. For the reason I have stated that is the reason why we believe we are right in standing by the Miners. That is why we are trying to do our best with cool heads and stout hearts to get this conflict through to a successful issue. While doing everything possible to bring about an early and honourable settlement, all the time that my Executive says that we must fight on, I will fight on with all my heart, all my soul, and all my strength.

Document 8

The Samuel Memorandum and related correspondence which is in the TUC Archives and can be found in many local trade union collections and the *British Worker*, 13 May 1926. There is also a copy in the National Museum of Labour History, NMLH/GS/SC13/003.

(a) A. Pugh
President, General Council
Trades Union Congress   May 12th, 1926

Dear Mr Pugh,

At the outcome of the conversations which I have had with your Committee, I attach a memorandum embodying the conclusions that have been reached.

I have made it clear to your Committee from the outset that I have been acting entirely on my own initiative, have received no authority from the Government, and can give no assurance on their behalf.

I am of opinion that the proposals embodied in the Memorandum are suitable for adoption and are likely to promote a settlement of the differences in the Coal Industry.

I shall strongly recommend their acceptance by the Government when the negotiations are renewed.

Yours sincerely,

(Signed) HERBERT SAMUEL

(b) Sir Herbert Samuel
London   12 May 1926

Dear Sir,

The General Council have carefully considered your letter of to-day and the memorandum attached to it, concurred in your opinion that it offers a basis on which the negotiations upon the conditions of the Coal Industry can be renewed.

They are taking the necessary measures to terminate the General Strike, relying upon public assurances of the Prime Minister as to the steps that we should follow. They assume that during the resumed negotiations the subsidy will be renewed and that the lockout notices to the Miners will be immediately withdrawn.

Yours faithfully

(Signed) ARTHUR PUGH, Chairman
        WALTER CITRINE, Acting Secretary.

(c) Memorandum

1. The negotiations upon the conditions of the coal industry should be resumed, the subsidy being renewed for such reasonable period as may be required for that purpose.

2. Any negotiations are unlikely to be successful unless they provide the means of settling disputes in the industry other than conferences between the mine-owners and they alone. A National Wages board should, therefore, be established which would include representatives of the two parties with a neutral element and an independent Chairman. The proposals in this direction tentatively made in the Report of the Royal Commission should be pressed and the powers of the proposed Board enlarged.

3. The parties of the Board should be entitled to raise before it any points they consider relevant to the issues under discussion.

4. There should be no revision of the previous wage rates unless there are sufficient assurances that the measures of reorganisation proposed by the

Commission will be effectively adopted. A Committee should be established as proposed by the Prime Minister on which representatives of the men should be included, whose duty it should be to co-operate with the Government in the preparation of the legislative and administrative measures that are required. The same Committee, or alternatively, the National Wages Board, should assure itself that the necessary steps, so far as they relate to matters within the industry, are not neglected or unduly postponed.

5. After these points have been agreed and the Mines National Wages Board has considered every practicable means of meeting such immediate financial difficulties as exist, it may, if that course is found to be absolutely necessary, proceed to the preparation of a wage agreement.

6. Any such agreement should

(i)   if practicable, be on simpler lines than those hitherto followed.

(ii)   not adversely affect in any way the wages of the lowest paid men.

(iii) fix reasonable wages below which the wage of no class of labour, for a normal customary week's work, should be reduced in any circumstance.

7. Measures should be adopted to prevent the recruitment of new workers, over the age of 18 years, into the industry if unemployed miners are available.

8. Workers who are displaced as a consequence of the closing of uneconomic collieries should be provided for by

(a) The transfer of such men as may be mobile, with the Government assistance that may be required, as recommended in the Report of the Royal Commission.

(b) The maintenance, for such period as may be fixed, of those who cannot be transferred, and for whom alternative employment cannot be found, this maintenance to compose in addition to the existing rate of unemployment paid under the Unemployment Insurance Act, of such an amount as may be agreed. A contribution should be made by treasury to cover the additional sums so disbursed.

(c) The rapid construction of new houses to accommodate transferred workers. The Trades Union Congress will facilitate this by consultation and co-operation with all those concerned.

Document 9

The *British Worker*, 14 May 1926, provided several accounts of victimisation and why there was no return to work. The three extracts below are indicative of its views and concerns.

(a)   WHY WORK DID NOT BEGIN
       Employers Make Fresh Attack upon Trade Unionism & Workers'
                              Standard of Life
                          MILLIONS STILL OUT

There was a general expectation on Wednesday, when the Great Strike terminated, that work would be resumed forthwith. To the great disappointment of the nation this did not happen.

Many men who went to work were told they must accept fresh conditions and lower wages. Upon instructions from their Unions they refused to do this, and were thereupon told their employers did not want them.

The situation is thus a very difficult one still – and made more so by the fact that while, during the strike all those out were in good humour, large numbers are indignant at this new attack on Trade Unionism.

(b)   STAND TOGETHER
Fellow Trade Unionists,

The General Strike has ended. It has not failed. It has made possible the resumption of negotiations in the coal industry, and the continuance, during negotiations, of the financial assistance given by the Government.

You come together, in accordance with the instructions of the Executive of your Unions. Return together on their instructions, as and when they are given.

Some employers will approach you as individuals, with the demand that you should accept conditions different from those obtaining before the stoppage began.

Sign no individual agreement. Consult your union officials and stand by their instructions. Your Union will protect you, and will insist that all agreements previously in force shall be maintained intact.

The Trade Union Movement has demonstrated its unity. That unity remains unimpaired. Stick to your Unions.
                          GENERAL COUNCIL,
                            TRADES UNION CONGRESS

(c)   NO VICTIMISATION
Those employers who imagine that the calling off of the General Strike means the collapse of the Trade Union Movement are making the mistake of their lives.

Many are trying to impose vindictive terms on the workers; they are trying to compel men to sign humiliating documents; they are trying to beat down wages.

If they persist they will find out how mistaken they are. They will find the spirit of the British worker is not only unbroken, but unbreakable.

Further, these employers, in addition to making a mistake, are breaking an obligation of honour.

The General Council, by calling off the General Strike, made the way clear for an honourable peace. It did so on the understanding that the spirit of its action would be reciprocated by the other side. It did so in reliance on the public assurances of the Prime Minister that he would foster the spirit of peace.

The calling off of the strike was not evidence of weakness. It was evidence of the genuine belief that peace could be obtained on terms honourable and beneficial to the whole Movement and the whole nation.

The General Council responded to the Prime Minister's appeal. Much depends upon how far he is prepared to back up the speech by action. If he will use all his influence to see that no employer tries to victimise and humiliate the workers, then peace may be saved. If not . . .

Let there be no mistake. The Trade Union Movement is not suing for mercy. It is not beaten. It is not broken. Its strength is unimpaired and even reinforced by the solidarity which the response of the General Strike has revealed. If one class of employers, misinterpreting and calling off the strike, thinks it can seize the opportunity to disrupt and degrade the Trade Union Movement, the situation is grave indeed. To that the Movement cannot and will not submit.

The alternative – the only alternative – to that grave situation is peace: peace honourably made and, on both sides, honourably kept.

Document 10

Memorandum of a Special Meeting held at 35 Parliament Street, SW1 at 6.0 p.m. on Thursday, 13 May 1926 between the representatives of the railway companies and the representatives of the trade unions, including Sir Felix Pole for the Great Western Railway, C.T. Cramp for the NUR, J. Bromley for ASLEF and A.G. Walkden for the RCA. There is a copy of this in PRO, RAIL 786, 6.

[Sir Felix Pole began by suggesting that the railway companies had been badly hit by the strike and that the men had broken their contract. In reply to Bromley's request for a return to work based upon seniority he replied in the following manner with the following responses.]

Sir Felix Pole replied that the guiding principle will be that the Companies will call upon men as and when the work admits and in accordance with seniority on each grade at each station or depot, and that it is not the intention to promote men from one grade to another as suggested. . . . With regard to the first condition of the Notice, Sir Felix Pole explained that it is considered the men, by going on strike, have committed a breach of their contract with the Companies under which a month's notice should be given on either side. The Government had publicly notified that 'arrears of wages claimed by certain employees on strike or absent without leave in respect of work already performed will be subject to deduction equivalent to the amount of wages for the period of the notice required and not given by such employers' and the Companies consider they are legally entitled to call upon all strikers to forfeit a week's pay at normal rates. They also feel very strongly that the breach of Agreement should carry with it some penalty.

Mr Bromley expressed the opinion that this would be regarded by the men as fine.

Sir Felix Pole replied that he hoped it would.

Mr Bromley explained that he was present at the meeting with a very contrite feeling for what had been done, but did not think it possible to get the men to return with these conditions. He also stated objection was taken to the document which is being presented to men offered re-instatement for signature.

Sir Felix Pole replied that the men were not being asked to sign the document. . . .

With regard to the several conditions of the Notice Sir Felix Pole explained that the Companies must examine certain cases where men or strikers had been guilty of acts of violence or intimidation, and they must reserve the right that any settlement should not apply to such persons.

Mr Bromley stated that such acts of violence would only have to be carried out in the heat of the moment, that intimidation was always a feature of any strike and begged that Companies should reconsider their decision in this respect. He pointed out that some of such men might actually be better servants than those who had stopped at work. . . .

Document 11

Details of the printing trade agreement from the *Morning Post*, 17 May 1926.

Terms of the Printing Trade
Freedom of Press to be Secured
No Interference with Contents

[This was arranged between Mr T.W. McAra of the Newspaper Proprietors' Association and Mr A.E. Holmes for the trade unions. It related to the London newspapers.]

1. There shall be no interference with the content of newspapers owned by members of the association.
2. There shall be no interference with or victimisation of any member of staff who worked or returned to work during the strike either in their own or another office, nor shall there be victimisation by the employers.
3. There shall be no interference by members of the Unions with the right of management to employ, promote or discharge members of staff. Nor shall it be necessary for print secretaries or managers of departments not engaged in production to be members of a Union.
4. No chapel meeting shall be held during working hours.
5. The strict observance of agreements in the Newspaper trades shall be regarded as a matter of honour affecting each individual employer and employee.
6. There shall be a joint committee of three from each side, which shall sit each day at three o'clock, to decide any case which may rise in connection with the above.
7. The evening paper will commence with the one o'clock edition. . . .

No re-engagement of any member of the regular staff will take place before 8 a.m.

Document 12

The terms of the return of the London dockers as reported in the *Morning Post*, 17 May 1926, a settlement that affected 50,000 men.

1. The Port Employers of London will re-engage labour on terms of the National Agreement which the Union admit they have broken.

2. . . . .

3. Employers will take as many men as work is available for.

4. . . . .

5. The Union undertake:

(a) Not in future to instruct their members to strike either nationally, sectionally or locally for any reason without exhausting the conciliation machinery of the National Agreement.

(b) Not to support or encourage any of their members who take individual action contrary to the preceding clause 5a.

(c) To instruct their members in any future dispute to refrain from any attempt to influence men in certain supervisory grades (to be specified later) to take strike action.

6. After general resumption of work any arrears of pay due to men at the time of the stoppage to be paid.

7. The Stevedores' Agreement of February 28 1924 is maintained. . . .

Document 13

PRO, RAIL 786, 6 General Managers' Memorandum, Great Western Railway, 19 May 1926

Number of Passenger, Milk and Perishable Trains

Day	Number of Trains	Total Mileage	Normal Mileage	% National Mileage
4	392	11,357	103,444	11.0
5	194	7,294	"	7.05
6	353	9,731	"	9.41
7	479	12,537	"	12.10
8	612	14,956	"	14.46
9	492	12,853	28,449	45.48
10	908	19,568	92,729	21.10
11	1,022	22,161	103,444	21.42
12	1,170	25,294	"	24.45
13	1,213	26,520	"	25.64
14	1,245	28,161	"	27.74

Document 14

PRO, RAIL 786, 6, Labour Report of the Great Western Railway to the Board from Sir Felix Pole, 21 May 1926

[The report indicated that 81 per cent of Great Western staff were on strike throughout the General Strike, that 5,620 staff were enrolled at Paddington and that 2,234 were used, with 2,200 special constables used throughout the system. From the first day of the strike volunteers were also trained as signalmen, being given two three-hour lectures.]

A textbook specifically prepared for such an emergency was used.

Altogether 252 volunteers were passed in effect to take charge of signal boxes and over 200 were sent to different boxes.

The London and North Eastern Railway Company indicated that they were seriously short of signalmen and 28 of the men trained in Great Western classes were supplied.

All volunteer signalmen performed their duties satisfactorily. . . .

Seven special trains were arranged for the conveyance of ocean passenger traffic and moved between London and Plymouth and all requirements were satisfactory made.

Special scheduled milk trains were run to London each day and the return of empty churns to the provinces was satisfactorily deals with. Prior to the strike an assurance was given to the Government that the company would do everything possible to handle milk traffic for London but, as an additional safeguard, the Government arranged for a large number of lorries to be sent into the country so as to be available in the event of any failure. It was soon demonstrated that the motor lorries were not required and they were kept back and utilised for other work. . . .

Freight Trains	Number of Trains	Total Mileage	% of Normal Mileage
		24 hours to 9 p.m.	
4 May	101	4,035	6.00
5 May	8	275	0.38
6 May	17	573	0.79
7 May	30	1,216	1.67

Freight Trains	Number of Trains	Total Mileage 24 hours to 9 p.m.	% of Normal Mileage
8 May	47	2,099	2.88
9 May	53	1,569	14.33
10 May	93	3,321	5.35
11 May	134	4,677	6.41
12 May	128	4,226	5.79
13 May	138	4,385	6.01
14 May	157	5,652	7.74

Document 15

Memorandum of 27 May 1926 between the Federation of Master Printers of Great Britain and Ireland, the Newspapers Society, the Master Bookbinders' Association (hereafter called 'The Employers' Organisation) and the Kindred Trades Federation . . . including London Society of Compositors, the Typographical Association, the Society of Women Employed in Bookbinding and Printing Trades, National Union of Journalists, PRO, LAB 27/9

IT IS AGREED

1. The Agreement between the printers which were in existence previous to May 1st 1926 shall remain in force. . . .

2. . . .

3. There shall be no lightening or sudden stoppage of work of any kind in the works of any member of the Employers' Organisation.

4. That Trade Unions agree that there shall be no interference with the contents of any newspaper, periodical, or other matter printed or published by members of the Employers' Organisation.

5. No chapel meeting to be held during working hours.

6. There shall be no interference with recognized apprentices in any trade dispute.

7. That Work and Departmental managers not engaged on production shall not be called out during any dispute. [There were also six other points listing restrictions imposed on the operation of the trade unions.]

Document 16

The TUC defended itself against charges of failure and betrayal in the General Council, *Report of the Conference of Executives of Affiliated Unions*, 25 June 1926 (London, TUC, 1926). It blamed the failure upon the intransigence of the leaders of the MFGB.

The General Council could not follow the Miners' Executive in the policy of mere negation. Such a course would have been to permit the splendid response of the sympathetic strike to evaporate by a process of attrition, which would have brought the unions to a position of bankruptcy, would have undermined the moral of the membership, and thus have destroyed their capacity to resist attempts that might be made to impose adverse conditions and general discrimination against the active membership when the industries directly engaged in the strike resumed their operations.

The Council were satisfied that, however long they continued the strike, they would still be in the same position so far as the attitude of the Miners' Executive were concerned, and consequently the Council was not justified in permitting the unions to continue their sacrifice for another day.

The strike was terminated for one sufficient reason only, namely that in view of the attitude of the Miners' Federation its continuance would have rendered its purpose futile.

BIBLIOGRAPHY

This is a brief list of sources and references most relevant to the study of the General Strike, the majority of which are referred to in this book.

Primary Sources

1. MANUSCRIPT SOURCES

Bevin, Ernest. Series of manuscript boxes, Archives of the TUC

Bradford Trades and Labour Council Archives on the General Strike, West Yorkshire District Archives, items 57 and 57/1

Citrine, Walter. 'Mining Crisis and National Strike', 4, 1, of the Diaries and Paper of Walter McLennon Citrine, Baron Citrine of Wembley, deposited in the British Library of Political and Economic Science

Duckworth, Henry. 'Dover Dockers. A Diary kept by one of them with Appreciation', now deposited in the British Library of Political and Economic Science, Coll. 0760

Eton College Wireless Bulletins

Gemmell, F. J. Collection of newspapers and other documents in the National Museum of Labour History

General Council of the TUC, Minutes

Liverpool Council of Action Collection

Miners' Federation of Great Britain, Minutes

NUR/GS, Head Office Circulars

PRO ADM 1/8697 for Fleet movements

PRO, WO 73/123 for Troop movements

PRO, CAB 23, Cabinet Conclusions

PRO, LAB 27, 9

PRO, RAIL 786, 6, 7

Samuel, Sir Herbert. Papers, House of Lords Library

Trades Union Congress General Council, SIC/20/1 1925–6, in the National Museum of Labour History, NMLH/GS/SCB/001–023, mainly of printed bulletins. NUR and railway lists and special bulletins produced throughout the country

Trades Union Congress, GS MD 26A, Committee of Arrangements

Trades Union Congress, MD 30 Supplementary List of General Council and Committee discussions, 1–4 May 1926

2. PARLIAMENTARY PAPERS, GOVERNMENT PUBLICATIONS AND GOVERNMENT RECORDS

Hansard

Macmillan Inquiry Report, HMSO, 1925

Ministry of Health, Circular 703
Report of the Royal Commission on the Coal Industry (1925), HMSO, Cmd 2600, 1926 (better known as
    the Samuel Report)

3. NEWSPAPERS, STRIKE BULLETINS AND PERIODICALS

Bedford Record
Bradford Worker
Brighton Bulletin
Brighton and Hove Herald
British Gazette
British Worker
Cricklewood and District Industrial Gazette
Daily Express
Daily Graphic
Daily Mirror
Dover and East Kent Worker
Dowsona Bulletin
Eccles Strike Committee Bulletin
Gloucester Strike Bulletin
Great Western Railway Bulletin
Illustrated London News
Labour Magazine
Lansbury's Labour Weekly
Leeds Mercury
Newcastle Workers' Chronicle
Peckham Labour Bulletin
Plebs
Preston Strike News
Railway Review
Scottish Worker
Sunday Pictorial
Sunday Worker
The Fascist Evening News
The Miner
The New Leader
The Northern Light
The Preston Strike News
The Reading Citizen
The Sketch
The Sphere
The Times
Tottenham Strike Bulletin
West Bromwich Free Press
Westminster Worker
Workers' Bulletin
Workers' Chronicle
Workers' Weekly
Yorkshire Observer
Yorkshire Telegraph

4. BOOKS AND TRACTS

Arnot, R.P. *The General Strike, May 1926: Its Origins and History*, Labour Research Department, 1926.

C.B. *The Reds and the General Strike: The Lessons of the First General Strike of the British Working Class*, CPGB, 1926

Bevin, E. *Trade Circular and the General Reporter of the AUBTW*, June 1926

Brown, T. *The Social General Strike*, London, 1926

Burns, E. *The General Strike (May 1926): Trades Councils in Action*, Labour Research Department, 1926

Cook, A.J. *The Nine Days: The Story of the General Strike told by the Miners' Secretary*, Miners' Women and Children, Cooperative Printing Society, 1926

Dutt, R.P. *The Meaning of the General Strike*, CPGB, 1926

Fyfe, H. *Behind the Scenes of the Great Strike*, Labour Publishing, 1926

Labour Party Conference, *Annual Report 1927*, Labour Party, 1927.

Postgate, R.W., Wilkinson E., and Horrabin, J.F. *A Workers' History of the General Strike*, Plebs League, 1927

Miners' Federation of Great Britain, *Statement on the General Strike of May 1926*, MFGB, 1927

National Union of Railwaymen, *Annual General Meeting (Weymouth), Tuesday, July 1926, Verbatim Report on the Proceedings in the General Strike*, NUR, GS, Head Office Circulars 1926

The General Strike: Extracts from Speeches by the Prime Minister and Winston Churchill, House of Commons, 3 May 1926, HMSO, 1926

The Secret History of the General Strike and the Blackleg State, reprint from *Lansbury's Labour Weekly*, 22 May 1926

TUC, *Annual Report*, TUC, 1927

TUC General Council, *The Mining Crisis and the National Strike 1926: Official Report* (Report of all Conferences), TUC, 1927

TUC General Council, *Mining Dispute National Strike*, Report of the General Council to the Conference of Executives of Affiliated Unions, 25 June 1926, TUC, 1927

5. ARTICLES

Wilkinson, Ellen. 'Ten Days that Shook the Cabinet', *Lansbury Labour Weekly*, pp. 8–11.

Secondary Sources

1. BOOKS AND PAMPHLETS

Arnot, R.P. *The Miners' Struggle: A History of the Miners' Federation of Great Britain (from 1910 onwards)*, 1953

Barnsby, G. *The General Strike in the Black Country*, Wolverhampton, The Wolverhampton, Bilston and District Trades Council, 1976

Bullock, A. *The Life and Times of Ernest Bevin I: Trade Union Leader 1881–1940*, Heinemann, 1960

Carter, P. and C. *The Miners of Kilsyth in the 1926 General Strike and Lockout*, Communist Party 'Our History' series, 1970

Citrine, W. *Men and Work*, Hutchinson, 1964

Clegg, H.A. *A History of British Trade Unionism since 1889, II, 1911–1933*, Oxford, Clarendon Press, 1985

Crook, W.H. *The General Strike: A Study of Labor's Tragic Weapon in Theory and Practice*, North Carolina, University of North Carolina, 1931

Davies, P. *A.J. Cook*, Manchester, Manchester University Press, 1987

Farman, C. *The General Strike, May 1926*, Rupert Hart-Davis, 1972

Hills, R.I. *The General Strike in York*, York, Borthwick Papers, 57, 1980

James, R.R. *Memoirs of a Conservative: J.C.C. Davidson's Memoirs and Papers 1910–1937*, Weidenfeld and Nicolson, 1969

Jones. T. *Whitehall Diaries II, 1926–1930*, ed. by R.K. Middlemass, Oxford University Press, 1969

Kibblewhite, L. and Ridgley, A. *Aberdeen in the General Strike*, Aberdeen, Aberdeen People's Press, 1977

Klugmann, J. *The History of the Communist Party, Vol. II*, Lawrence & Wishart, 1969

Lawson, Jack. *The Man in the Cloth Cap: The Life and Times of Herbert Smith*, Methuen, 1941

Laybourn, K. *A History of British Trade Unionism c. 1770–1990*, Gloucester, Alan Sutton, 1992

——, *The General Strike of 1926*, Manchester, Manchester University Press, 1993

Macfarlane, L.J. *The British Communist Party: Its Origins and Development until 1929*, MacGibbon & Kee, 1966

Maclean, J. *The 1926 General Strike in Lanarkshire*, Communist Party 'Our History' series, 1976

Mason, A. *The General Strike in the North East*, Hull, University of Hull, 1970

Morris, M. *The British General Strike 1926*, Historical Association, 1973

——, *The General Strike, 1926*, Journeyman Press, 1980

Peck, J.A. *The Miners' Strike in South Yorkshire 1926*, Sheffield, University of Sheffield Education Department, 1970

Phillips, G.A. *The General Strike: The Politics of Industrial Conflict*, Weidenfeld and Nicolson, 1976

Renshaw, P. *The General Strike*, Eyre Methuen, 1975

Skelley, J. (ed.) *The General Strike, 1926*, Lawrence & Wishart, 1976

Symons, J. *The General Strike*, Cresset Press, 1957

Trory, E. *Brighton and the General Strike*, Brighton, Crabtree Press, 1975

Turner, B. *About Myself*, Cayme Press, 1930

Union Place Community Resource Centre, *Nine Days, 1926: The General Strike in Southwark*, Southwark, 1976

Walentowicz, P.J. *The General Strike in Doncaster, May 1926*, Doncaster, Doncaster Library Service, 1986

2. ARTICLES

Baines, D. and Bean, R. 'The General Strike in Merseyside', in J.R. Harris (ed.), *Liverpool and Merseyside*, F. Cass, 1966

Foster, J. 'British Imperialism and the Labour Aristocracy' in J. Skelley (ed.), *The General Strike, 1926*, Lawrence & Wishart, 1976, pp. 3–57

Hastings, R.P. 'Aspects of the General Strike in Birmingham 1926', *Midland History*, II, pp. 250–73

Mason, A. 'The Government and the General Strike', *International Review of Social History*, 14 (1968)

Porter, J.H. 'Devon and the General Strike, 1926', *International Review of Social History*, 23, 3 (1978), pp. 250–73

Williams, A.R. 'The General Strike in Gloucestershire', *Transactions of the Bristol and Gloucestershire Archaeological Society*, 91 (1979), pp. 207–13

Woodhouse, T. 'The General Strike in Leeds', *Northern History*, 18 (1982), pp. 252–62

Wyncoll, P. 'The General Strike in Nottingham', *Marxism Today*, 16, June 1972

3. THESES

Clinton, A. 'Trades Councils from the Beginning of the Twentieth Century to the Second World War', unpublished PhD thesis, University of London, 1973

Scheps, A. 'Trade Unions and the Government 1925–7', unpublished DPhil thesis, University of Oxford, 1972

NOTES

INTRODUCTION

1. E. Bevin, *Trade Circular and the General Reporter of the AUBTW*, June 1926
2. Trades Union Congress General Council, *The Mining Crisis and the National Strike, 1926* (hereafter *The Mining Crisis and the National Strike*), section dealing with the Mining Situation: Report of a Special Conference of Executive Committees of Affiliated Unions held in Memorial Hall, Farringdon Street, London, on Thursday 29, Friday 30 April and Saturday 1 May 1926 (London, TUC, 1927), p. 35
3. K. Laybourn, *The General Strike of 1926* (Manchester, Manchester University Press, 1993)
4. *The Fascist Evening News*, 4 May 1926
5. E. Trory, *Brighton and the General Strike* (Brighton, Crabtree Press, 1975), pp. 7–8 deal with a public meeting held by the Brighton Fascists in Hove Town Hall, 20 March 1926
6. *The Sketch*, 12 and 19 May 1926
7. C. Wrigley, 'Trade Unionists, Employers and the Cause of Industrial Unity and Peace, 1916–1921', in C. Wrigley and J. Shepherd, eds, *On the Move: Essays in Labour and Transport History presented to Philip Bagwell* (London, Hambledon Press, 1991)
8. This was Sharpurti Saklatvala, MP. See R. Mace, 'The Strike in the Regions: Battersea, London', in M. Morris, *The British General Strike 1926* (London, Journeyman Press, 1980), pp. 379–93
9. *Yorkshire Factory Times*, 13 August 1925
10. R. Lowe, 'The Erosion of State Intervention in Britain, 1917–24', *Economic History Review*, 31, 1978, pp. 270–86; R. Lowe, 'Government and Industrial Relations, 1919–1939', in C.J. Wrigley, ed., *A History of British Industrial Relations, II, 1914–1939* (Brighton, Harvester, 1987). See also J.A. Jowitt and K. Laybourn, 'The Wool Textile Dispute of 1925', *Journal of (Regional and) Local Studies*, 2, 1, Spring 1982
11. R.R. James, *Memoirs of a Conservative: J.C.C. Davidson's Memoirs and Papers 1910–1937* (London, Weidenfeld and Nicolson, 1969), ch. 8.
12. F. Wilkinson, 'Collective Bargaining in the Steel Industry in the 1920s', in A. Briggs and J. Saville, eds, *Essays in Labour History 1918–1939* (London, Croom Helm, 1977)
13. TUC Standing Orders, 1921
14. TUC, *Report*, 1924
15. Jowitt and Laybourn, 'The Wool Textile Dispute of 1925', *Journal of (Regional and) Local Studies*, 2, 1, Spring 1982
16. *Report of the Royal Commission on the Coal Industry (1925)* (London, HMSO, Cmnd 2600, 1926), p. xi, pp. 232–7
17. P. Davies, *A.J. Cook* (Manchester, Manchester University Press, 1987), p. 91
18. Minutes of a meeting between the Mining Association and the MFGB, 26 March 1026, BP, D.3, 13, pp. 223–55
19. A. Mason, 'The Government and the General Strike', *International Review of Social History*, 14, 1968
20. A.M. McIvor, 'Essay in Anti-Labour History', *Society for the Study of Labour History, Bulletin*, 53, 1, 1988
21. D.E. Baines and R. Bean, 'The General Strike in Liverpool', in J.R. Harris, ed., *Liverpool and Merseyside* (London, F. Cass, 1966), p. 254
22. Public Record Office, Cabinet Papers, Cab 81 (26)
23. *Labour Gazette*, September 1925
24. W. Citrine Papers, W. Citrine, 'Mining Crisis and National Strike', 4 January 1926

25. *Ibid.*, 28 February 1926
26. *Ibid.*, 3 March 1926
27. J.H. Thomas, *My Story* (1937), pp. 105–6
28. TUC General Council, *Report of Proceedings at a Special Conference of Executives*, 20 January 1927; W.H. Crook, *The General Strike: A Study of Labor's Tragic Weapon in Theory and Practice* (North Carolina, University of North Carolina, 1931), pp. 311–12
29. Emile Burns, *The General Strike (May 1926): Trades Councils in Action* (Labour Research Department, 1926)
30. Crook, *The General Strike*, p. 413
31. On 11 May 500,000 copies were produced in London, 40,000 in Cardiff, 30,000 in Glasgow and 70,000 in Manchester
32. Interview with Mr Skinner, a retired power worker who worked at a power station in Barnsley during the General Strike, conducted by Keith Laybourn in 1979; *The Illustrated London News*, 15 May 1926
33. *The Sphere*, 8 May 1926
34. PRO, Cab 29/260 ST (24) 23rd Meeting, 14. Cab 27/331, S.T. Bull, 10 May
35. *The Illustrated London News*, 8 May 1926; *The Sphere*, 8 May 1926
36. PRO, Cab. 23/331, S.T. Bull, 10 May
37. H. Duckworth, 'Dover Dockers', p. 8. The manuscript is in the special collection in the British Library of Political and Economic Science
38. A photograph of some of the volunteer student dockers at Dover is reproduced in the *Daily Mirror*, 15 May 1926
39. *British Gazette*, 8 May 1926
40. TUC, *Mining Crisis and the National Strike*, p. 34
41. *British Gazette*, 12 May 1926
42. *Daily Graphic*, 13 May 1926
43. *Nine Days 1926: The General Strike in Southwark* (Southwark, Union Place Community Resource Centre, 1976), pp. 39–40
44. James, *Memoirs of a Conservative*, p. 242, quoting from J.C.C. Davidson's draft memoirs
45. *British Gazette*, 13 May 1926
46. James, *Memoirs of a Conservative*, pp. 246–9
47. *The Times*, 11 May 1926
48. Public Record Office, RAIL 786, 6

49. *Ibid.*, General Managers' Meeting with the Minister of Transport, 11 May 1926
50. *Ibid.*, including the *Great Western Railway Bulletin*, no. 5, 9 May 1926. It was produced at Paddington station
51. *Ibid.*, *Great Western Railway Bulletin*, no. 9, 12 May 1926. On 6 May there were 353 trains, and on subsequent days 479 (6th), 479 (7th), 612 (8th), 908 (10th) and 1,072 (11th)
52. *Ibid.*, Rail 786, 7, Chief of Police, Daily Report
53. *Ibid.*, Rail 786, 7, Labour Report, 21 May 1926 on the General Strike
54. Burns, *The General Strike (May 1926): Trades Councils in Action*
55. *Ibid.*, chap. 4
56. *Lansbury's Labour Weekly*, 22 May 1926
57. A. Clinton, 'Trades Councils from the Beginning of the Twentieth Century to the Second World War' (unpublished PhD thesis, University of London, 1973), p. 214, quoting *Town Crier*, 11, September 1925 and Bradford Trades and Labour Council, *Yearbook 1926*, p. 3
58. Clinton, 'Trades Councils', p. 23
59. Burns, *Councils in Action*, ch. 4
60. The National Museum of Labour History, 103 Princess Street, Manchester
61. C.B., *The Reds and the General Strike: The Lessons of the First General Strike of the British Working Class* (London, CPGB, 1926)
62. Burns, *Councils in Action*, p. 76
63. *Ibid.*, p. 76; J. Maclean, *The 1926 General Strike in Lanarkshire* (London, Pamphlet 65, Our History, CPGB), p. 10. The Lanarkshire Joint Committee of the Council of Action had contact with twenty-three councils of action in Lanarkshire and was connected with the General Council of the Scottish Trades Union Congress, which had overall control of the General Strike in Scotland
64. Scottish Trades Union Congress, *Daily Bulletin*, no. 2, 6 May 1926, quoted in Maclean, *The 1926 General Strike in Lanarkshire*
65. *Scottish Worker*, no. 1, Monday 10 May 1926
66. Burns, *Councils in Action*, p. 80; A. Mason, *The General Strike in the North East* (Hull, Hull University Press, 1970), pp. 22–5

67. T. Woodhouse, 'The General Strike in Leeds', *Northern History*, 18, 1982, pp. 252–62

68. P. Wyncoll, 'The General Strike in Nottingham', *Marxism Today*, 16, June 1972

69. R.P. Hastings, 'Aspects of the General Strike in Birmingham 1926', *Midland History*, II, p. 256

70. A.R. Williams, 'The General Strike in Gloucestershire', *Transactions of the Bristol and Gloucestershire Archaeological Society*, 91, 1979, pp. 207–13; D.E. Baines and R. Bean, 'The General Strike of Merseyside' in J.R. Harris, ed., *Liverpool and Merseyside* (London, F. Cass, 1966); Hills, *York*

71. *Scottish Worker*, 10 May 1926, also quoted in Liz Kibblewhite and Andy Ridgley, *Aberdeen in the General Strike* (Aberdeen, Aberdeen People's Press, 1977), p. 11

72. TUC General Council Intelligence Committee, Report of a visit to York and Doncaster by W. Paling, 11 May 1926, quoted in P.J. Walentowicz, *The General Strike in Doncaster, May 1926* (Doncaster, Doncaster Library Service, 1986), p. 6

73. Letter from Walter Barber, secretary of Bradford Trades Council, to Walter Citrine, 21 May 1926, West Yorkshire District Archives, Bradford, items 57 and 57/1, 56D8/10/4; *The Bradford Worker*, 8, 11 and 13 May 1926, WYDA, Bradford, 56 D8/1/4

74. Hills, *York*, p. 14; Baines and Bean, 'Merseyside', pp. 248–51

75. J.H. Porter, 'Devon and the General Strike, 1926', *International Review of Social History*, 23, 3, 1978, p. 355; PRO, Rail 786, 6 and 7 indicates this in the general managers' reports and the *Great Western Railway Bulletin*

76. R.W. Postgate, Ellen Wilkinson and J.F. Horrabin, eds, *A Workers' History of the Great Strike* (London, Blackfriars Press, 1927), pp. 28–32

77. *British Worker*, 5 May 1926

78. *Ibid.*

79. PRO, Cab/ 27/260, ST 24/25, 9 May 1926

80. Burns, *Councils in Action*, p. 143

81. Walentowicz, *General Strike in Doncaster*, p. 12, which also draws on TUC files, 11 May 1926; *Doncaster Gazette*, 14 May 1926

82. James, *Davidson*, p. 227

83. *Yorkshire Observer*, 9 May 1926

84. *Workers' Weekly*, 21 May 1926

85. *British Gazette*, 6 May 1926; *Daily Express*, 10 May 1926

86. Cook, *The Nine Days*, pp. 17–18

87. *Ibid.*, pp. 18–24

88. *Workers' Bulletin*, 13 May 1926

89. *Hansard*, 13 May 1926

90. Citrine, *Men and Work*, pp. 144–5; General Council, *Mining Dispute*, 1927, p. 21

91. Citrine, 'Mining Crisis and the National Strike, 11 May 1926'; Citrine, *Men at Work*, pp. 200–1

92. The Anti-Socialist Union Press Service, no. 5, 12 May 1926

93. TUC General Council, *Report to the Conference of the Executive of Affiliated Unions, June 25, 1926* (London, TUC, 1926), p. 26

94. *The Miner* (organ of the Miners' Federation of Great Britain), 4 June 1926

95. Samuel Papers (House of Lords Record Office) A/66, Pugh to Samuel, 18 May 1926; *Observer*, 23 May 1926

96. Letter from the TUC General Council to all Secretaries of Affiliated Trade Unions and for the Information of Trades Councils and Strike Committees, 12 May 1926

97. R.P. Hastings, 'Aspects of the General Strike in Birmingham, 1926', *Midland History*, II, p. 268

98. *Morning Post*, 17 May 1926

99. *Ibid.*

100. PRO, Rail 786, 6, Memorandum of a Special Meeting held at 35 Parliament Street, SW1, Thursday 13 May 1926

101. *Ibid.*, Memorandum of a Special Meeting held at 35 Parliament Street, 14 May 1926, at which J.H. Thomas MP was present.; *British Worker*, 15 May 1926.

102. *Ibid.* Other meetings between the railway companies and the rail unions, on 20 and 21 May, 2 June and 2 July, reveal that the unions felt that the employers were continuing to victimise those who had gone on strike. Indeed, J.T. Cramp argued on 2 July that this action was directly contrary to the settlement

103. See *The Miner* from June to November 1926. This traces the changing patterns of negotiations and noted on 6 November

1926 that Russia had sent £986,000 to
the British miners in twenty-five weeks

104. *Workers' Bulletin*, 13 May 1926

105. Cook, *Nine Days*, p. 23

106. M. Jacques, 'Consequences of the
General Strike', in J. Skelley, ed., *The
General Strike, 1926* (London, Lawrence
and Wishart, 1976), pp. 375–7; A.
Bullock, *The Life and Times of Ernest
Bevin: I, Trade Union Leader 1881–1940*
(London, Heinemann, 1960), p. 345; P.
Renshaw, *The General Strike* (London,
Eyre Methuen, 1975), p. 250

107. TUC General Council, *Report of the
Proceedings at a Special Conference of Trade
Unions, 20–21 January 1927* (London,
TUC, 1927), pp. 4–5, 21–7, 42–3, 45

108. Labour Party Conference, *Annual
Report 1929* (London, Labour Party,
1929), p. 92

TUESDAY TO FRIDAY, 27–30 APRIL 1926

1. PRO, Cabinet Conclusions, Cab. 23, Cab
19 (26), 28 April 1926 at 11.30 a.m.

2. PRO, LAB 27/9

3. National Museum of Labour History,
NMLH/GS/SCB/001, GS 3–10,
referring to SIC/20/1/1925–6

4. TUC, *The Mining Situation* (London,
TUC, 1926), particularly paragraphs 4, 6,
9, 11, 12 and 15

5. Trades Union Congress General Council,
The Mining Situation (London, TUC,
1926)

6. PRO, LAB 27/9

7. TUC, *Mining Situation*

8. PRO, LAB 27/9

9. W. Citrine, 'Mining Crisis and National
Strike', p. 162 from 4, 1 of the Diaries
and Papers of Walter McLennon Citrine,
Baron Citrine of Wembley, deposited in
the British Library of Political and
Economic Science

10. General Council of TUC, 'Proposal for
Co-ordinated Action', put to the trade
unions on 30 April 1926 and adopted 1
May, in TUC General Council, *The
Mining Crisis and the National Strike*
(London, TUC, June 1927), p. 31; see
Selected Documents

SATURDAY 1 MAY 1926

1. This, and the subsequent extracts, are
taken from *The Mining Crisis and the
National Strike* (London, TUC, 1927),
which includes *The Mining Situation:
Report of a Special Conference of Executive
Committees of Affiliated Unions held at
Memorial Hall, Farringdon Street, London,
on Thursday, April 29th, Friday, April 30th
and Saturday, May 1st, 1926*

2. MFGB, Special Conference, 30 April,
Report (London, MFGB, 1926), p. 34

3. TUC/GS MD 26A, Committee of
Arrangements; MD 30 Supplementary
List of General Council and Committee
discussions, 1–4 May

4. PRO, LAB 27/9; also PRO, CAB 23,
Cab 21 (26), 2 May 12 noon

5. *The Mining Crisis and the National Strike*,
p. 10

6. Citrine, *Men and Work*, pp. 165–6

7. National Museum of Labour History,
archive on the General Strike

SUNDAY 2 MAY 1926

1. A.J. Cook, *The Nine Days: The Story of the
General Strike told by the Miners' Secretary*,
(London, Miners' Women and Children
Fund, Co-operative Printing Society), p. 16

2. General Council, Minutes, 2 May 1926

3. PRO, CAB 23, Cab 21 (26), 2 May 1926,
12 noon

4. PRO, LAB 27/9

5. PRO, CAB 23, Cab. 21 (26), 2 May
1926, resumed meeting at 9.30 p.m.

6. Bevin Series Box 3, C2/2 15 and 16

7. R.R. James, *Memoirs of a Conservative:
J.C.C. Davidson's Memoirs and Papers
1910–1937* (London, Weidenfeld and
Nicolson, 1969), pp. 233–4

MONDAY 3 MAY 1926

1. General Council, *Mining Dispute*, pp.
11–13; Citrine, *Men and Work*, p. 171;
General Council, Minutes, 2–3 May 1926

2. *Daily Mail*, 3 May 1926, Manchester
edition

3. PRO, LAB 27/7

4. PRO, LAB 27/9, Appendix H

5. *The General Strike* (London, HMSO,

1926), extracts from the speeches by the prime minister and Winston Churchill in the House of Commons, 3 May 1926

6. *Hansard*, 3 May 1926
7. James, *Davidson*, p. 236
8. PRO, RAIL 786,7 Wireless Broadcast Messages, 3 May 1926
9. PRO, RAIL 786, 6, 3 May letter from C.T. Cramp of the NUR to Sir Felix J.C. Pole, general manager of the Great Western Railway, Paddington station, W2
10. PRO, RAIL 786, 6, extract from Notice to All Staff

TUESDAY 4 MAY 1926

1. Cook, *Nine Days*, p. 16
2. In PRO/LAB 27/9, reported in various newspapers and TUC archives
3. James, *Davidson*, p. 240
4. PRO, RAIL 786,7 Wireless Broadcast Messages, 1 p.m. 1926
5. PRO, RAIL 786, 6
6. PRO, RAIL 786,6, Chief Officers' Conferences, GWR
7. Citrine, *Men and Work*, p. 183
8. *The Times*, 4 May 1926
9. H.H. Fyfe, *Behind the Scenes of the Great Strike* (London, *Daily Herald*, 1926), p. 26
10. *The Fascist Evening News*, 4 May 1926
11. H. Duckworth, 'Dover Dockers, A Dairy kept by one of them, with Appreciation', now deposited in the British Library of Political and Economic Science

WEDNESDAY 5 MAY 1926

1. TUC, General Council, Minutes, 5 May 1926
2. PRO, LAB 27
3. *Yorkshire Telegraph*, 5 May 1926
4. Ministry of Health, *Circular 703*
5. PRO, CAB 23, Cab 29/260 ST 23rd meeting, 14 Cab 27/3322 S.T. Bull., 10 May 1926
6. G.A. Phillips, *The General Strike: The Politics of Industrial Conflict* (London, Weidenfeld and Nicolson, 1976), pp. 163, 210
7. *Hansard*, 5 May 1926
8. PRO, CAB 23, Cab 24 (26), 5 May 1926 at 11.0 a.m., also referring to Cab 21 (26), Appendix II
9. Quoted in the *British Worker*, 6 May 1926

10. Quoted in *Tottenham Strike Bulletin*, 5 May 1926
11. Fife, *Behind the Scenes*, pp. 34–5; Citrine, *Men and Work*, pp. 181–2

THURSDAY 6 MAY 1926

1. Phillips, *General Strike*, p. 185
2. *British Gazette*, 6 May 1926
3. *Hansard*, 6 May 1926
4. PRO, LAB 27/9, 24–27, Appendix K
5. *Nine Days in 1926: The General Strike in Southwark* (Southwark, Union Place Community Resource Centre, 1976), pp. 47–8
6. Kibblewhite and Ridgley, *Aberdeen in the General Strike*
7. PRO, RAIL 786, 6 Chief Officers' Conference of the Great Western Railway, 6 May, 10 a.m.
8. *British Worker*, 6 May 1926
9. *Cricklewood & District Industrial Gazette*, No. 1, 6 May 1926
10. Duckworth, 'Dover Dockers', p. 4
11. *Ibid.*, p. 8
12. *British Worker*, 6 May 1926
13. *Tottenham Strike Bulletin*, 6 May 1926

FRIDAY 7 MAY 1926

1. *British Gazette*, 7 May 1926
2. *West Bromwich Free Press*, 7 May 1926
3. PRO, CAB 23, Cab. 25 (26), 11 a.m., 7 May
4. PRO, CAB 23, Cab. 52/25 (26)
5. *British Worker*, 8 May 1926
6. The *Scottish Worker*, 10 May 1926, refers to the fact that 120 people were arrested as a result of rioting in the Glasgow East End on Wednesday, Thursday and Friday
7. *Ibid.*, 7 May 1926
8. *Gloucester Strike Bulletin*, 8 May 1926
9. Liverpool Council of Action, collection
10. General Council, GC 131, 13/7/11, Soc. minutes, 8 May 1926

SATURDAY 8 MAY 1926

1. *Daily Express*, 10 May 1926; Eton College Wireless Broadcast, No. 10, Monday 10 May 1926
2. *British Gazette*, 8 May 1926, whose circulation reached 836,000

3.   *Yorkshire Observer*, 9 May 1926
4.   *British Worker*, 8 May 1926
5.   Citrine, *Men and Work*, p. 187
6.   PRO, CAB 23, Cab. 27 (26), 8 May 1926, 6 p.m.
7.   The more precise content of the final version is presented, in part, in the section dealing with 12 May 1926
8.   *Tottenham Strike Bulletin*, 8 May 1926
9.   *The Northern Light*, 8 May 1926

SUNDAY 9 MAY 1926

1.   *British Gazette*, 10 May 1926
2.   *Wigan Strike Bulletin*, 9 May 1926
3.   *British Worker*, 9 May 1926
4.   PRO, LAB 27/9, Appendix M
5.   Citrine, *Men and Work*, p. 194
6.   Extract from a letter, 11 May 1926, sent to Branch and Strike Committee Secretaries by the National Union of Railwaymen, Unity House, Euston Road, London
7.   *British Gazette*, 10 May 1926
8.   Cook, *Nine Days*, p. 18
9.   Special London edition of the *Peckham Labour Bulletin*, no. 3, 9 May 1926; the *Bradford Worker*, 11 May 1926

MONDAY 10 MAY 1926

1.   Citrine, *Men and Work*, pp. 194–5
2.   General Council, *Mining Dispute* (1927), p. 21
3.   *Daily Graphic*, 11 May 1926
4.   Eton College Wireless, Monday 10 May, 7 p.m., no. 11
5.   PRO, CAB 23, Cab. 28 (26), 10 May at 4 p.m.
6.   PRO, LAB 27/9 and the *British Gazette*, 10 May 1926 (now with a circulation of 1,127,600). The latter report suggested that the London, Midland and Scottish had 1,000 trains running, the London and North Eastern, the Great Western 800 and Southern Railways 900
7.   *British Worker*, 10 May 1926
8.   TUC, 'Where We Stand', *British Worker*, 10 May 1926
9.   *Preston Strike News*, 10 May 1926; *Scottish Worker*, 10 May 1926

10.   PRO, CAB 23, Cab. 28 (26), 10 May at 4 p.m.

TUESDAY 11 MAY 1926

1.   Eton College Wireless Bulletin, Monday 11 May, 7 p.m.
2.   T. Jones, *Whitehall Diaries, Vol II, 1926–1930*, ed., R.K. Middlemass (London and Oxford, Oxford University Press, 1969), p. 42
3.   Cook, *Nine Days*, p. 15
4.   Citrine, *Men and Work*, pp. 200–1
5.   J. Simon, *Three Speeches on the General Strike* (1926), Appendix III
6.   *British Worker*, 11 May 1926
7.   National Museum of Labour History, NMLH/GS/SCB/002, extract from the Official Bulletin of the Trades Union Congress, no. 8 11/5/26
8.   NUR, General Strike News Bulletin, Tuesday 11 May 1926
9.   PRO, LAB 27/9 and General Strike collection in the National Museum of Labour History
10.   *Scottish Worker*, 11 May 1926; *Preston Strike News*, 11 May 1926; *Reading Citizen*, 11 May 1926
11.   E. Trory, *Brighton and the General Strike* (Brighton, Crabtree Press, 1975), p. 14, with eye-witness accounts from p. 25
12.   Eton College Wireless Bulletin, no. 13, 11 May 1926 at 4 p.m., W/GSL/23 xxiv
13.   PRO, RAIL 786/6, 11 May 10 a.m.
14.   PRO, LAB 27/9
15.   *The Times*, 11 May 1926; PRO, CAB 23, Cab. 29 (26), 11 May 1926 at 6 p.m.

WEDNESDAY 12 MAY 1926

1.   Cook, *Nine Days*, p. 22
2.   PRO, LAB 27/9 Appendix N, extracts from the Full Official Report of Proceedings at Downing Street on Wednesday 12 May at 12.20 when representatives of the General Council announced the calling off of the General Strike
3.   B. Turner, *About Myself* (London, Cayme Press, 1930), p. 312
4.   PRO, LAB 27/9
5.   PRO, CAB 23, Cab, 30 (26), 12 May 1926 at 2.30 p.m.

6. Eton College Wireless Bulletin no. 15, 4 p.m., 12 May 1926
7. PRO, RAIL 786, 6 Notes on Meeting [of Railway Companies and the Minister of Labour] in the Minister of Labour's Rooms, House of Commons, 9.30 p.m., 12 May 1926
8. PRO, LAB 27/9, 26/9. Also PRO, RAIL 786, 6 indicates in the Chief Officers' Conference of the Great Western Railway, held at 10 a.m. on 12 May that the situation was improving and that there were 357 sets of engineers available on Tuesday and even more for Wednesday
9. The full details appear in the Appendix, and the full terms of the Samuel Memorandum appeared in the *British Worker*, 12 May 1926, evening edition. The National Museum of Labour History, NMLH/SC13/003 contains a copy of the above letters and Memorandum
10. A full and accurate copy of this statement, put out on 12 May, appears in the *GEC Bulletin*, no. 10, p. 5, 13 May 1926, NMLH/GS/SCB/004
11. *Tottenham Strike Bulletin*, 12 May 1926
12. *Ibid.*
13. *Doncaster Gazette*, 14 May 1926
14. *Workers' Bulletin*, 12 May 1926
15. The *East London Observer*, 13 May 1926

THURSDAY 13 MAY 1926

1. *Trades Union Congress: Official Bulletin Issued by TUC General Council*, no. 10, 13 May 1926
2. *British Worker*, 13 May 1926
3. PRO, RAIL 786, 6, General Managers' Meeting, letter from the NUR dated 13 May 1926 from C.T. Cramp
4. PRO, RAIL 786, 6, Memorandum of a Special Meeting held at 35 Parliament Street, SW1 at 6 p.m. on Thursday 13 May 1926, between representatives of the Railway Companies and the Railway Trade Unions
5. *Hansard*, 13 May 1926
6. *TUC: Official Bulletin Issued by the General Council*, no. 10, 13 May 1926
7. *Hansard*, 13 May 1926; PRO, LAB 27/9

8. PRO, RAIL 786, 7, Wireless Broadcast Messages, 13 May, 1 p.m.
9. *Workers' Bulletin*, 13 May 1926
10. Cook, *Nine Days*, p. 23
11. Citrine, *Men and Work*, p. 198

FRIDAY 14 MAY 1926

1. *Bradford Pioneer*, 14 May 1926
2. *Bradford Worker*, 14 May 1926
3. *Ibid.*
4. *British Worker*, 15 May 1926; PRO, RAIL 786, 7
5. *Railway Review*, 14 May 1926
6. PRO, RAIL 786, 7, Wireless Broadcast, 14 May 1926, 1 p.m., quoting the Statement of Electric Railway House
7. PRO, LAB 27/9, Agreement regarding the London County Council Train Service, signed 14 May 1926
8. *British Worker*, 15 May 1926, referring to the Eccles Strike Committee; *Scottish Worker*, no. 5, 14 May 1926
9. *Daily News*, 15 May 1926; MFGB, *Annual Report*, 1926

SATURDAY TO FRIDAY, 15–21 MAY 1926

1. *Daily Mirror*, 15 May 1926
2. Reproduced in the *British Worker*, 15 May 1926
3. PRO, LAB 27/9, Agreement in General Printing Trades, signed 15 May 1926
4. PRO, LAB 27/9, 50–53
5. *British Worker*, 17 May 1926
6. *Morning Post*, 17 May 1926; Selected Documents
7. PRO, LAB 27/9 contains the copy of the London Newspaper Agreement signed 20 May 1926 and a Memorandum, 27 May 1926, between the Federation of Master Printers of Great Britain and Ireland, the Newspaper Society, the Master Bookbinders' Association (hereafter 'The Employers' Organisation') and the Printing and Kindred Trades Federation including the London Society of Compositors, the Typographical Association, the Society of Women Employed in the Bookbinding and Printing Trades, the National Union of Journalists [and other groups]

8. PRO, RAIL 786, 6, Details of a Meeting between the Railway Companies and the Railway Unions held 20 May 1926

9. *Railway Review*, 21 and 28 May 1926

10. PRO, RAIL 786, 6, Memorandum of a Meeting between the Railway Companies and the Railway Unions, at 3 p.m. on Friday 21 May 1926 [43 pages long]; Memorandum of a Meeting between the Railway Companies and the Railway Unions, 2 June 1926; Memorandum of a Meeting between the Railway Companies and the Railway Unions, 2 July 1926

11. General Council, 129, 13/7/1, Bevin to Firth, 29 May; TGWU GEC Minutes, Report of Sub-Committee on the General Strike

THE RECKONING

1. P. Davies, *A.J. Cook* (Manchester, Manchester University Press, 1987), pp. 11–14, 194–207

2. Miners' Federation of Great Britain, *Annual Report, 1926*, p. 445

3. Jones, *Whitehall Diaries*, 31 May 1926, p. 60

4. PRO, CAB 23/53, 38 (26)

5. C. Farman, *The General Strike, May 1926* (London, Rupert Hart-Davis, 1972), p. 253

6. Jones, *Whitehall Diaries*, pp. 68–9

7. MFGB, EC minutes, 20–21 September and the letter of Evan Williams to Winston Churchill, 13 September 1926, quoted in MFGB, Minutes, 1926, pp. 774–5

8. MFGB, Minutes, 1926, p. 1037

9. TUC General Council, *Report of Proceedings at a Special Conference of Trade Unions, 20–21 January 1927* (London, TUC, 1927), pp. 4–5, 21–7, 42–3, 45

INDEX